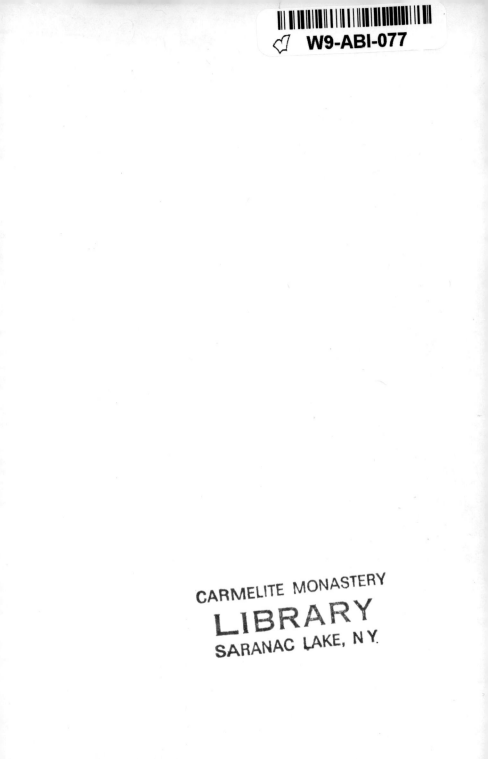

OPEN SPIRIT

OPEN SPIRIT

LADISLAUS BOROS

Translated by Erika Young

Grateful acknowledgment is made for material abridged from pp. 19-20, 22-23, 32, 34, and 37 of *Hymn to the Universe* by Pierre Teilhard de Chardin, translated by Simon Bartholomew, copyright © 1961 by Editions du Seuil, copyright © 1965 in the English translation by William Collins Sons & Co. Ltd. and Harper & Row, Publishers, Inc.; also from pp. 122 and 123 of *Letters from a Traveler* by Pierre Teilhard de Chardin, © 1962 by Harper & Row, and about 280 words from *Let Me Explain* by Pierre Teilhard de Chardin, edited by Jean-Pierre Demoulin, © 1970 by Harper & Row.

Published originally as *Denken in der Begegnung*, ©1973 by Walter-Verlag AG, Olten. Published in Britain by Search Press, London; English translation © 1974 by Search Press Limited.

ISBN: 0-8091-0194-7 (cloth)
ISBN: 0-8091-1856-4 (paper)

Cover design by Morris Berman

Published by Paulist Press
Editorial Office: 1865 Broadway, N.Y., N.Y. 10023
Business Office: 400 Sette Drive, Paramus, N.J. 07652

Printed and bound in the United States of America.

Contents

Foreword

This book began as a kind of balance sheet, drawn up for myself alone. I had the chance to spend some months entirely on my own, undisturbed. I decided to use the time to examine the influences that had formed my ideas.

First of all I asked myself about the experiences and events in my life that had affected me most deeply. I found that I had taken over countless ideas, consciously or unconsciously, from other people—so much so that I attribute the formation of my mental landscape, in second place, to them.

Therefore I also had to describe my 'intellectual encounters'. And so the book took its present form. In it I examine the ideas I hold, and give some account of those people who have helped to shape them.

In it, too, I hope to show at last that 'small area of fruitfulness' in which I can live out my human existence—despite all the dangers that lie in wait for the questing mind.

Perhaps some people will find no point in a stranger's attempts to take stock of himself. Nevertheless I feel I owe it to my friends, the readers of my works, to place these thoughts of my solitude before them.

It is not presumption that leads me to make these pages public. I hesitated for a long time before doing so, because

I began this book for myself alone and always intended it thus. That is why there are no footnotes, and only citations in the text. As to publishing the book, I acted on the—I hope appropriate—advice of friends whose opinion on the matter differed from my own.

But I must make one thing clear from the start. I have not listed *all* the ideas that have influenced me, or all my 'intellectual encounters'. Two of these seem to me overwhelmingly important: the meeting with Jesus Christ that determined the future course of my life and left its mark on me forever; and that with Ignatius Loyola, to whom I owe a great deal of what I am today. And I do not specifically mention such thinkers as Plato, Leibniz, Pascal, Kierkegaard, Newman, Thérèse of Lisieux and Dostoievsky, to mention only a few who have been vital to my intellectual development.

In this book I have tried to concentrate on essentials with that openness of spirit that I have always striven for. But even here some of my readers will be dissatisfied. Openness of mind is a great virtue which really enables us to face up to reality. But at times we have to summon up the courage to reach decisions, despite the burden of uncertainty, obscurity and danger. That is not dishonest so long as men, finite and time-bound, never forget in reaching their decisions that they *are* finite.

Basically, I ask myself in this book whether my life can be true for others; that is to say, whether my own experiences can be useful to my friends, and whether I can pass those experiences on to them.

Socrates and honesty

Socrates and honesty

I should like to make 'honesty' the measure of all true thought. In the terminology once current and now coming into its own again, honesty meant to speak, act and behave so that you could always give public account of your words, deeds and attitudes. When I began to study my intellectual formation, I discovered how hard it was really to live like that.

I am aware, too, that a spurious honesty can be very dangerous. That consists in persuading yourself that an intellectually honest man does not commit himself, tries to avoid all error by making no ultimate choices, and turns the weakness of indecisiveness into a strength which is just scepticism without any illusions. That's a long way from intellectual honesty.

Honesty of mind obviously means avoiding prejudgements. An intellectually honest man will categorically refuse to put reality into the framework of any preconceived scheme. And that brings me to something else—something I have always tried to realize in myself—the quietness of contemplation.

The intellectually honest man is open to all truth, wherever it may appear. He is ready to listen. But that means he doesn't reject anything in advance, doesn't consider anything to be intrinsically impossible, and won't let himself be influenced by preconceived ideas.

I don't know if many people, especially in ecclesiastical circles, would agree with this view. Anyway, it's how my own mind works.

Intellectual honesty, therefore, demands a questing mind —one that probes and tests as though to say: 'If you're out to convince me, take care; I'm going to look at your arguments very closely indeed'.

A necessary part of such an attitude is the honest man's readiness to admit he has been in error. He certainly won't use untenable arguments in self-defence. In *Thus Spake Zarathustra* Nietzsche described the requisite attitude thus: 'I seek a genuine man, a proper, simple man, a man of one meaning and of all honesty, a repository of wisdom, a saint of knowledge, a great man!'

That is why an honest man is often a very slow thinker. When he begins to think, he tries to forget everything he has previously known. What he aims at as a thinker is the greatest possible spontaneity and originality.

An honest man also realizes that basically he knows very little. And of this little he has only tested and verified a small part for himself and his friends. So he gives himself and them time to study and mature—*tempo galant 'uomo*—as the Italians put it so exactly.

He wants to produce from himself, for himself and others, only what is 'crystal-clear'—and by that he means what has been experienced to the full, what Paul Valéry has called *midi le juste*—brightness without shadow. This attitude somehow reminds me of the blueness of the Mediterranean—translucent air, clarity, and through it all, in it all, the radiance of the Godhead.

Newman was able to depict this same attitude by means of images and examples that fitted his northern European background more exactly. He described it as the attitude of a 'gentleman'. In the eyes of the Church the same attitude of decency, honesty and openness to truth and life leads to that sacramental conferring of baptism which we call 'baptism of desire'—an ugly term, I think. Surely it would be better to call it something like 'baptism of longing' or, quite simply, the 'sacrament of honesty'?

An intellectually honest man, then, is one who doesn't make up his mind in advance; he probes and tests; he realizes that he knows very little, and that he must stand back respectfully to make way for the truth. When I think of these qualities, my mind automatically turns to Socrates —a man who has deeply influenced my attitude to life. With his help, I shall try to describe what I mean by intellectual honesty.

In the year 399 BC a man named Socrates stood trial in Athens. He was accused of the most serious crime possible at that time—it was said that he sought to overthrow the traditional religion of the people and was corrupting the young. Socrates was condemned to die by his own hand. Even though some friends gave him opportunities to escape, he was resigned to the death that awaited him.

Socrates is one of the few honest men whose life, and not least whose death, decisively influenced the history of the West. What has still to be accomplished in us, in the innermost depths of each and every one of us, was foreshadowed in him. He was the progenitor of the Western world—a world torn by the same contradictions that were part of his own life and death. Do with me what you will—'if you can catch me before I give you the slip' —those were among his last words before he died.

Socrates forced his fellow citizens to use their minds.

This seems an innocent enough activity on the surface. Nevertheless it caused some of the people to rise up against him. It was inevitable that he would arouse disapproval by his quiet way of questioning adults in public, and making young people laugh at their elders' ignorance, mock them and force them to admit that they just didn't know. Still worse was the fact that young people began to imitate Socrates by asking their own questions to embarrass their elders.

And so Socrates was accused of corrupting the young. We have to understand the accusation correctly. They accused him not of teaching the young evil ways, but of destroying their good ways. Somehow he managed to teach them to disrespect their elders. In his school they learnt not to be influenced by anyone. They also learnt not to accept received opinions and beliefs without examining them closely.

For an Athenian that was a serious charge. If young people began to question traditional beliefs in the light of intellectual evidence, the rights of the individual would come to have priority over those of the state. And Socrates' evil influence lay precisely there.

Hence he was not merely a disturber of the peace—he was a non-believer. If he had taken money from his teaching, as the Sophists did, he would have been able to reach only a handful of people—those who could pay. And things would not have been so bad. But he taught everyone, young and old alike. And his teaching was free.

I shall return to the accusation of irreligion in a moment. But first of all I want to give a brief sketch of Socrates the man.

As a person he was simple and all of a piece. I think

of him as having an enormous forehead, a broad face, prominent eyes, thick lips and a flat nose. He probably neglected his appearance a bit and made people smile at him. But he had robust health and did not tire easily. In the Dialogues we see him as a man who can drink endlessly, without getting drunk. He stops teaching only when his last listener has fallen flat on his back.

Socrates' mental processes were equally remarkable. If Plato is to be believed, he could think for hours on end, remaining quite motionless. Once he stood for a whole day and night, in front of witnesses. He remained perfectly still and didn't even blink. At dawn he pulled himself together, bathed, and joined the crowd, as he usually did.

In general he was fairly strict with himself, but was no ascetic. He didn't interfere with others' entertainment. Surrounded by a group of young people whose morals were by no means exemplary, he refused to let himself be influenced by them. He joked about immorality, yet Plato's reports show that he firmly condemned it.

As a citizen, Socrates seems to believe strictly in obedience. But you feel all the time that his submissiveness resembles Pascal's; there is something behind it: it grows out of an even deeper lack of respect. There must be laws, he seems to say. Society could not exist without them. And it is clearly desirable that those laws should be sensible ones. But even when they are ridiculous, there is positive value in their mere existence. They protect us from anarchy. Such smiling conformity has something splendidly arrogant about it.

Lastly, was Socrates really a religious man? I shall deal with this question more fully later. At this point I shall say only that he was a profoundly moral man. An inner voice spoke to him whenever he had to refrain from some action. And he listened to that voice. He spoke of it as a 'spirit'—as though it were a guardian angel. Oddly enough this voice only spoke negatively. It did not say what was good and should be done, but only what was bad. From every point of view Socrates was a remarkable human being.

His teaching method, too, was extremely curious. This by no means ordinary man walked calmly about the streets of Athens, surrounded by a group of young men. He wouldn't let them call him 'Master'. Nevertheless they were passionately devoted to him. His teaching was as unfettered as his walking.

Once they were in the gymnasium where athletes rubbed themselves with oil and showed off their muscles. Another time they walked by the river Ilyssos, or strolled along a street, or found themselves in the market place, or in a shop. All places were good for talking. The Socratic dialogue was never a monologue.

Socrates was always asking small, insignificant questions, rather like an examining magistrate trying to elicit the truth from the accused. The art of the Socratic dialogue is characterized by two elements—irony and maieutics.

Socratic irony has little or nothing to do with what is meant by the word irony today. There was no frivolity about it. In essence his irony consisted in admitting his own ignorance. For example Socrates wanted to talk about justice. But instead of speaking of it as an abstract concept, he let his followers tell him about it. He pretended to understand nothing, or almost nothing, of what they said to him. He affected not only ignorance but even, at times, plain stupidity. I can imagine how he must have laughed to himself when some naïve young man believed his pretence.

Socratic irony has a two-fold advantage in philosophical discussion. In the first place there is the advantage in putting yourself on the defensive from the start. How can you reproach a man for his ignorance when he has already cut the ground from under your feet by his own admission of it? There is no greater advantage than to be unable to lose. People are often anxious only because they're proud. Socratic irony is very relevant to this, and has always been an example to me in my own thinking.

But irony also has the advantage of attack. Under the guise of pretended ignorance, Socrates was able to ask all those simple questions which are, as I have often found for myself, the most tricky. He could ignore traditional ideas without being suspected of scorning them. But, more important, he was able to force his pupils' minds back to very basic intellectual positions. There are things you can understand only if you want to—but if you don't want, then you simply don't understand. And Socrates almost always refused to understand the explanation he was given. Hence his questioning was often extremely painful: 'Why?', 'Wherefore?', and 'Explain it to me, please'.

To irony Socrates added his own special brand of dialogue, which he called *mäeutik*. The word means 'assistance at the birth'. Socrates often said that he fulfilled the same function in the world of the intellect as his mother did in daily life. He believed that everyone bore all knowledge within him, and all that was needed was help in bringing it out into the light of day. Questions aid the birth of thought.

But there is something even more important here. If

questions are put carefully and logically, they enable you to arrive at the truth by yourself, without having to get ideas from outside.

I shall now consider the purpose of the Socratic dialogue with its two elements of irony and *mäeutik*. What theses did it enable Socrates to propound? If I simply listed the individual items that made up Socrates' ideas, I should not be describing the part he played in Western thought. Socrates' importance is not only in his thought and ideas.

His primary importance is that he stood at the end of an intellectual tradition which had started long before his own time, but had almost at once begun to develop on the wrong lines. It was high time for it to be superseded, and that is precisely what Socrates did by leading philosophy by a roundabout way into entirely new country.

That was his first and primary service to the West. The second lay in the manner and method of his philosophical thinking, which led him to the discovery of totally new problems. He was able to provide a fresh starting-point for philosophy and guide it this time in the right direction. But I must briefly explain these two statements. I feel they are of special relevance today when we too find ourselves in what is perhaps a similar intellectual situation.

The history of Greek philosophy up to the fourth century was essentially a 'search for a way'. The philosopher who in my view stands at the beginning of this philosophy is Pythagoras. In his time philosophy was still part of natural science. The Greek philosophers concentrated on the visible world and looked for its component parts or elements. These they found in air, water, earth and fire, either on their own or in combination.

Pythagoras found himself face to face with this tradition. He was a mathematician, one of the first to have considered the mathematical characteristics of geometrical shapes. We all know the theorem of the right-angled triangle. But not so many know that Pythagoras moved on to solid geometry.

At that time there were no Roman or Arabic numerals. Counting was done in points. For Pythagoras, material objects were constructed according to numbers which expressed their nature.

He was not merely a mathematician but a musician. One afternoon while walking in the town he noticed three smiths hammering a piece of iron in their workshop, and he became aware of a series of intervals in the sounds he heard—intervals which we call fourths, fifths, octaves. These different sounds were due to the different weights of the hammer blows.

Pythagoras' discovery also pointed to modern physics and astronomy, and in this regard there is nothing to criticize in it. It makes perfectly good sense to say that numbers as such cannot form bodies, but that 'Pythagorean numbers' combine to make invisible matter visible. That is the definition of the atom. And so we reach the atomic principle.

Democritus also held that matter was formed out of precisely such invisible yet solid units—atoms. What distinguishes them from one another is the manner and method in which they combine. It exactly resembles the way in which all words in our language are formed from its twenty-six letters.

Atomism was subsequently taken over by Epicurus and Lucretius. It remained part of philosophy for a long time, and of physics still longer. With atomism, pluralism seems to have gained the upper hand.

But Parmenides—we are still in the fifth century BC—disagreed profoundly. He thought it absurd to say that the world consisted of atoms. His argument is very simple and at the same time subtle. It runs as follows: If the universe is made up of indivisible atoms, there must be space between them. But space is nothingness. One would therefore have to say that nothingness also exists. But that is intellectually meaningless. 'Above all, my son,' said old Parmenides to one of his pupils, 'I forbid you to say that nothingness exists. Be unshakable and assert: Being is, and non-being is not. There is no third alternative.'

Zeno affirmed Parmenides' teaching still more strongly. He pointed to the contradictions that resulted from the belief that the world was made up of atoms: Either the atoms are divisible, or they are indivisible. If they are indivisible, they touch one another. But if they touch one another, they are one. If they become one, bodies are infinitely small. Or otherwise atoms are divisible. But in that case they are extended. If they are extended, they are themselves composed of atoms, of extended atoms. In that case individual bodies are infinitely large. How can one decide this question? By pointing to experience? No, Zeno emphatically declares. The philosopher's task is not to gather experiences but to question them, to 'ask for their credentials'. To this day no one has found a totally satisfactory answer to his paradox.

Greek thought was as though transfixed before this intellectual impasse. It was not yet sufficiently mature to find a way out. Fortunately the Sophists now made their appearance. I do not think there is any need for me at this stage to try to rehabilitate them. They certainly were not—as people believed for a time—corrupters of minds or exponents of absurd doctrines. In reality they held no doctrines—and were proud of it. Their rôle in the history of Greek thought was—so far as I can tell—to 'train' the Greek mind, to introduce it to dialectics, and to work out the basic principles of logic.

If, for example, a man like Georgias boasts that he can prove that nothing whatever exists, one must not be so naïve as to think that he believed his own proof or thought he could make others believe it. But his subtlety, his mental pyrotechnics and word-play amused the Greek mind. And that was a good thing at the time.

It still is. When a pupil comes up against a seemingly insoluble problem, it does him no good endlessly and at all costs to persevere with it. Better perhaps is what a kind friend can do for him—take him on a beautiful walk, show him lakes and mountains. If Georgias can prove that nothing whatever exists, it simply means that nothing can be proved.

This was the moment—we are now in the fourth century before Christ—that Socrates appeared. He was certainly no friend of the Sophists, whose play with words had to come to a stop if philosophy was to progress. But, in a manner of speaking, he too was a Sophist. He destroyed the old dogmatism. By guiding Greek thought away from metaphysics and in the direction of inner observation or, if you like, existentialism, he introduced a completely new element into it, and this is where his real significance lay. The maxim of the dogmatists was—'Know the world'; and of Socrates —'Know yourself'.

Socrates, whose intention it was to create a practical

philosophy, did not allow these philosophical attempts to degenerate into rejection of all speculation. He was not interested in Empiricism, still less in moral teaching. He did not confine himself to saying, 'Be just', but asked, 'What is justice?' That is to say, he was looking for definitions or, to put it differently, for the 'essence' of things. Thus he created the right climate for the appearance of Plato, and still more of Aristotle.

In order to give a definition of, say, 'justice' or 'cleverness', Socrates invented a form of induction. First he collected individual examples and then tried to find their common characteristic. In the case of justice, he began by considering the principal qualities possessed by a just man. When he had found these, he tried to 'abstract' the common element, and this would be the essence of justice. Everything that does not belong to the essence is chance or accident.

We also say: It is essentially characteristic of the just man that he does not lie to his friends, does not steal and does not hurt them. But it is an accidental attribute, it is chance, that he has, say, fair hair or is plagued by rheumatism. All that seems, and is, very simple. But it was by means of such simple ideas that Socrates—without perhaps being aware of it—created for philosophy a new point of departure, and opened up new possibilities of progress.

Once you recognize the 'essence' of things, then concrete objects themselves appear as 'incarnations' of this one essence. The individual object participates in the universal. Once you have grasped the universal, you can say, for example, that an individual man is clever. What you are saying is that this man realizes within himself the idea of cleverness, or participates in the idea of cleverness.

While Socrates walked about the *Agora*, paying ironic compliments and putting subtle questions, a young man was passionately listening and entering into his mind— Plato. This young man had, perhaps, a less 'beautiful' soul and was less deeply anchored in morality, but certainly possessed a more powerful intelligence and showed himself more eager to attack.

After the death of his master—indeed during his life-time—Plato himself started to construct at first shorter dialogues, then longer ones, in which he demonstrated Socrates' teaching. At the beginning these dialogues (of the first period) scarcely strayed from Socrates' own teach-ing. As long as he was alive, Plato remained a submissive pupil. But as he matured, he was no longer content to repeat his master's teaching. He tried to deepen it.

With his first intellectual probing, a serious problem emerged: If ideas, the things objects have in common, are universal and unchangeable, then they are necessarily 'external' to those objects which, in our experience, are always unique and changeable. Justice is distinct from the just man. But if the things of our experience are as they are, and at the same time part of an idea, then ideas are 'more real' than reality itself. How is this to be explained?

Certain difficulties, three in number, arose from this argument. First: what are ideas in themselves, and how are we to think of them? Second: where are they? And third: what is the relationship between them and concrete reality? These three problems appear in almost all Plato's Dialogues. He seems to have been obsessed by them. But let me imagine him speaking for himself. Plato would ascribe the difficulties to Socrates: '*Socrates*: Things are, my gifted friend, as we have said, what they are through their participation in an idea. White things are white, because they participate in whiteness. Is it not so? —*Entiches*: Absolutely, Socrates!—*Socrates*: But whiteness in itself, what is it? What statements can we make about it? Can we say, perhaps, that it is round?—*Entiches*: No, we cannot say that, Socrates!—*Socrates*: Or that it is square?—*Entiches*: We should have no grounds for saying that!—*Socrates*: Has it shape of any kind?—*Entiches*: One cannot say that it has shape. There is no reason for it to have one shape rather than another. It is simply white! —*Socrates*: But—if it has no shape, no dimension and no weight—whiteness is simply not real. It does not exist. But you will straightaway reply: If whiteness as such does not exist, white objects—which are white because they partake of whiteness—are not white at all. Should we say, Entiches, that white things are not white?— *Entiches*: We should not!—*Socrates*: If white objects are really white, and if they are white because they partake of whiteness, then whiteness exists after all!—*Entiches*: That must be so.—*Socrates*: Whiteness therefore exists, and it does not exist, at the same time! How can we escape from this dilemma?'

These problems gave rise to the controversy over universals, as it was called in the Middle Ages. Plato was not able to suggest a satisfactory solution. At a later date Aristotle, too, concerned himself with it. He (and all the Scholastics) were to continue Plato's ideas by dealing with his three problems in a way essentially unchanged since then. Satisfactory answers to these questions have not been forthcoming right up to present-day Idealism.

While I am on the subject of these 'historical' considerations, I must briefly refer to the source of our information about Socrates. The extent of our ignorance of this man remains a scandal in Western history. We know practically nothing about him, and what we do know is coloured by the subjective accounts of three individuals.

In the year 423 Aristophanes put on a comedy during a feast in honour of Dionysius. His play, *The Clouds,* received third prize. The story centres upon a farmer and his son, and begins in the early morning. The farmer cannot sleep on account of his debts, and of his son. His mind turns to Socrates, who is to teach him how to get rid of his creditors without paying his debts. From his conversation with Socrates we learn that the latter wants to destroy the farmer's illusory belief in the gods. He attributes the absolute power of the highest god, Zeus, to natural events. Aristophanes wanted to depict Socrates as a destroyer of the old mythology. It is quite possible that the impression made by this play influenced his unfortunate trial in the year 399.

Xenophon gives a very different picture of Socrates. Xenophon was a prosperous landowner. He loved hunting and horses, had a distinguished wife who was devoted to him, and well-brought-up children. How should we think that such a man would understand an 'outsider' like Socrates? Without intending to, he conventionalized him. For Xenophon Socrates was simply a good, a very good man, who could, however, have been less abrupt with his judges and come to some arrangement with them, in order to avoid having to drink the poison.

But the real evidence, in my view, comes from Plato. It is true, of course, that one can discuss endlessly how much of himself Plato put into his description of Socrates. But the Socrates whom he re-created is an apt and historically very probable human being. Even if not every detail is factually correct, Plato's version replaces the historical Socrates with advantage. At any rate, his is the Socrates we know and have to deal with. We must try to understand and—I hope—love him.

And now we are in a position to ask what grounds there were for the accusation brought against Socrates that he was a destroyer of traditional religion.

It was said of him that he did not believe in the gods. To understand what was meant by this, we must first establish that he was an adherent of the religion of Apollo. The commitment to truth of Socrates, and the clarity, the orderliness associated with Apollo, match one another. Hence the Delphic priesthood acquired a powerful advocate in the very midst of a philosophical movement that was otherwise opposed to the old religion.

According to Plato's *Apology* the question posed by Socrates in Delphi was one of alternatives. 'Is there one wiser than Socrates?' By '*sophos*' was meant in the fifth century BC the turn of the mind that made a man ask philosophical questions. The Pythia's answer No, that no one was wiser, made Socrates the wisest of the philosophers. But this meant that in the eyes of all Greece his allegiance was to Delphi. Hence the religion of Apollo won for itself a priest among the philosophers and here, at any rate, was a case of mythology entering into partnership with the new ideas.

That puts Socrates very far from being an unbeliever. But I must tread carefully here. Greek, as distinct from modern, atheism did not consist in the denial of all and every divine being, but only in a freedom of obligation towards the reigning gods and legends. Nor did the new philosophy deny the existence of God. On the contrary, it claimed to have a more accurate idea of the being of the Godhead than the traditional myths and cults. Socrates was obliged to give his allegiance to both the old and the new ideas, and paid with his life for his witness to the new.

I shall now append—without further commentary—the final lines of Phaedo's Dialogue about the death of Socrates:

'How shall we bury you?' [asked Crito]. 'Any way you please,' [said Socrates, laughing gently], 'if you can catch me before I give you the slip.' . . . With these words he rose from the couch and went into another room to bathe . . .

Thereupon Crito nodded to the slave-boy who was standing by. The lad went out and came back after some considerable time with the man who was to administer the poison, which he had brought ready mixed in a cup. When Socrates saw him he said: 'Well, my good man, you know all about this business; what must I do?'

'Nothing,' he replied, 'except drink the poison and keep walking about until your legs feel heavy; then lie down, and the poison will do its own work.'

So saying he held out the cup to Socrates. He took it, and very gently, Echecratos, without a tremor or a change of colour or expression, but looking up at the man with open eyes as was his wont, said: 'What do you say about pouring a libation to some deity from this cup? May I, or not?'

'Socrates, we prepare only what we think is a sufficient dose.'

'I understand,' said he, 'but I may and must pray to the gods that my departure hence be fortunate. So I offer that prayer and hope it may be granted.'

With these words he raised the cup to his lips and calmly drained it, without a murmur. Until then most of us had just managed to restrain our tears; but as we watched him drink the poison we could do so no longer. I could not repress a flood of tears . . . 'What strange behaviour, my friends,' he said. 'My chief reason for sending away the women was to prevent them from behaving in this absurd fashion.' . . . Socrates continued walking up and down. At length he said his legs were feeling heavy, and lay down on his back . . . Then the man felt him again, and said that when the lack of sensation reached his heart he would be gone . . . Socrates, uncovering his face, which had been veiled, uttered his last words: 'Crito, we owe a cock to Asclepius. Be sure to pay the debt.'

'That,' said Crito, 'shall be done. Have you anything else to say?'

There was no reply but after a little while the attendant uncovered him; he wore a fixed stare. Crito, seeing this, closed his mouth and eyes. (*The Trial and Death of Socrates*, Everyman edition [London, 1963], pp. 171–5.)

The man condemned as unbeliever died obedient to the god Apollo. His last words were a request for a service to the healing god Asclepius. But Plato's very last words about his death, whose meaning is inexhaustible, were these: 'Such was the end, Echecratos, of our friend, who was surely the best and most upright man of any we have ever known.'

I think the story of Socrates gives some idea of what I mean by intellectual honesty—a virtue essential for all intellectual work, and a necessary prerequisite for an honourable future for us all.

Irenaeus and patience

Irenaeus and patience

The virtues of mildness and resignation were not, God knows, given me in the cradle. Yet now I think one of the most beautiful statements of personal witness are Augustine's words to his opponents, the Manicheans: 'Those who don't know sighs and tears may be angry with you . . . And those who have never been led astray. But I can't be angry with you. On the contrary, we shall look together for what is equally unknown to us both. Neither of us shall be so bold and arrogant as to assert he already possesses the entire truth.'

Vital patience is a far-reaching, reconciling power. By means of it contradictions are resolved in a mysterious way. It enables man, burdened at all levels by his personal history of good and evil, to acquire that all-embracing resignation which not only removes the contradictions in his life but accepts life's apparent meaninglessness and gives it a curious right to exist.

Patience expects only good from life, but is not surprised by its opposite. Herein lies the power of resignation. Life must be accepted for what it is. Its hardships, quirks and mysteries must not be turned into their opposites. Only the clarity of the known and the darkness of the unknown can give us the hidden meaning of life. Seldom or never have I been able to laugh at the strangeness of human existence, and still more seldom could I view it with contempt. But it confirmed me in my own personal contradictions.

This setting a value on life, this giving oneself and others time for growing and testing, must not be confused with the attitude that gives up the struggle for beauty and goodness in advance, because it is not aware of their importance.

But a patient man is also an exceptionally receptive one. And this very receptivity tells him how little he can achieve by himself: how deeply he and others are involved in the uncontrollable chaos of interconnexions that make up this world.

What is real lies on the further side of what we have perceived, produced and thought out for ourselves; on the further side, too, of our discoveries and errors. The real meaning of human existence is not what has already been accomplished but what remains to be done—something which we, for good or ill, cannot control by ourselves.

In this connexion it seems important to consider the life, person and significance of Irenaeus of Lyons. Which of us can put ourselves into the shoes of this solitary Greek from the Gaul of the second century after Christ? But there are events full of marvels for those able to open their eyes to them, and which enable them in a special way to become spokesmen of the future.

Here is a man living in primitive Christian times who has given us our freedom today. Our Christian destiny was to a large extent decided long ago by him. Since Irenaeus' spiritual struggles were very similar to the struggles going on in my own life, and those I have observed in many of my friends, I thought it necessary to examine one aspect of the life of this man in search of God : the inner darkness that comes upon a believer's life.

There can be times in our personal quest for salvation when every movement of our soul as it strains upwards to the spiritual heights seems void of meaning. It would be dishonest of me not to admit this. It is a matter of losing touch with God. Historically Irenaeus found himself in just such a spiritual situation. If I am fully to pay tribute to his achievements, I must first think back to the story of my own relation with God, its course, and the paths it took.

At that time, in the days of my later youth, I lived unthinkingly for each day, unaware of those inner powers of transformation that were already at work within me. Perhaps there was in my soul a longing for higher things, a nobility of attitude, a fellowship with beauty—for all at once I felt myself drawn by the powers of the Absolute. That was my first movement towards God— my conversion. A mysterious flame began to burn in my life. A marvellous brightness filled the first days of my conversion to God. It was the gaiety of heart that writers on the spiritual recognize as an infallible sign of the soul's movement towards God. It put me at that height of intensified living which theologians in the Middle Ages described as 'out of the body'—the intense concentration of the spirit on higher things.

Evil crept near in the same unobservable way. Suddenly I found that I could no longer endure such grandeur of being. That beauty and delicacy of perception filled me with a dismay I had not so far been aware of. Dark powers made themselves felt in me—self-seeking and self-flattery made all previous experiences worthless. My life suddenly

B

ceased to radiate happiness. From one moment to the next my joy changed to disillusion—my world became empty and despairing: full of spectres and devoid of consolation.

Perhaps such a transformation of the entire being does not happen to everyone. It is certainly a very painful experience. Once it has happened, you can no longer see the things of the world as harmless. Fate—or perhaps God—can throw you from deepest bliss into profoundest gloom, from first love into almost uncontrollable aversion. The days pass. The powers of inner movement have been exhausted. The way to God is blocked.

In such a moment everything, heaven itself, seems touched by evil. *And God does not speak.* His silence seems to say that he is powerless. Uncertainty creeps into the soul. What is true and what false, what good and what evil? Unspeakable horrors crowd in on all sides.

This is what happened when evil became alive in me. It was as though a final horror was still to come. Suddenly everything became false and so unbelievably distorted that it all seemed to speak of life unredeemed.

Hence it is possible in life to have a God and a living soul, to belong to them, to rejoice in them, to suffer as a result of one's relationship with them, and then to say there is no God and no soul. Man's powers of denial are boundless.

Who has not experienced these heights and depths of a life lived for God? Christ's life, too, was filled with such contradictory experiences, to the point where his sweat fell like great drops of blood upon the ground. Redemption means detaching oneself from the heights *and* the depths of life, and saying: 'All this is transitory and does not touch on the real essence of my relationship with God.'

This, then, is what courage means, courage for life, for real living. The essence of the virtue of courage doesn't lie in attack, self-reliance or anger, but in patient endurance. That is so not because patience and endurance are better and more perfect in themselves than active self-reliance, but because the real world is made up of contradictions to the point where man can only call on his greatest and deepest powers of soul on occasions of such seriousness that no possibility of struggle remains, and there is nothing left save endurance. Patience is very different from the passive acceptance of all evils that come. Aquinas wrote: 'The patient man is not one who doesn't see evil, but one who doesn't let it force him into sadness.' To be patient means not to let one's soul be robbed of its gaiety and clarity of vision by the sufferings that are part of the working out of salvation.

If life in all its dimensions, both happiness and pain, is not accepted with patience, there arises a situation of ultimate godlessness. This does not mean that God's existence is expressly denied. Indeed, such a state of mind can be accompanied by great piety and devotion, but only in times of light, joy and happiness. Piety and devotion are absent in moments of darkness, misfortune and sadness.

What that means is that God no longer rules over the totality of a man's life. A man in that state runs from everything that signifies a final decision for God. He can no longer find God in the superficial meaninglessness of the world and of his own life. He can no longer talk with God about the great things of the creation story: 'And God saw everything that he had made, and behold, it was very good' (Gen. 1.31). When a man can no longer say these words, he is faced by an ultimate abyss between the realities of the world, and God. He no longer lets God 'reign'; he rejects God's darkness, banishes him to the light areas of creation, and does not lay bare to him his own deepest depths. He no longer possesses an all-powerful Lord but only a poor little weak 'Other' who can be of no help to him in those important areas of his life, his sufferings.

That was the spiritual situation of the early Christians of the second century. The first glow of readiness for sacrifice, of a still chronological closeness to God, had begun to wane. The expectation of an early return of Christ in glory had shown itself to be false. Christians found themselves once more in a world that turned its back on their belief in the good. And there grew up an aversion to the Christian God which was not to be repeated until our own day.

The ordinary people, it is true, remained faithful to their suffering Saviour; ordinary people always understand more about the pain of living than do the more learned, whose education often turns to their disadvantage. God is especially close to simple people living out their life amid the pains and shocks of daily life. Their life is wholly enclosed, in good fortune and misfortune, by a boundary wall whose other side is God.

At about the same time there emerged a group of people who were no longer prepared to worship a God who allowed suffering, darkness and perplexities, a God who entered into the darkness of human life by himself becoming man. Historically this movement came to be known as 'Gnosticism', from 'gnosis', the teaching of the enlightened ones. Those who gave the movement its decisive impetus were perceptive, cultivated men. They knew all the tensions of actual life: its contradictions, hardships and intellectual problems. They experienced the good in a very positive way, especially in its existential form—the nobility, purity and beauty of existence. They found themselves given over to the demands of the spirit, above all in the highest matters, in their ideas. Their attitude made them very vulnerable, so that they were inclined to see all imperfections as threats, and to equate them with evil.

Imperfection, they taught, has no right to existence. Suffering they saw as a power, a reality determining life, something living, the opposite of God. It was necessary, they believed, to withdraw from everything that existed in the dark sphere of the world, from sin and weakness, to condemn it, and to remain pure and perfect. There was no room for mercy. Only one thing was necessary in the world—to set free the real man, this creature of light fallen into darkness, to deliver him from his darkness and to set one's face against all forms of mildness and compassionate understanding. The bent rod must be broken and the flickering flame extinguished. In a world of the pure, illumined by the light of the spirit, these had no right to life.

Nor can a Christ be God who places himself at the side of the weak and oppressed, who helps the sick and blesses the little ones, who has such compassion on human suffering that it forces tears into his eyes, who feels deeply with his threatened creatures. That kind of Christ is not God.

Christ (so the Gnostics thought) is a pure creature of light and there is no weakness in him. God is beautiful, always brings joy, is always turned towards the pure. He has nothing to do with sinners who stop his glory breaking through in the world. Such people belong to the sphere of Satan, and must be damned, banished, so that creation can raise itself to God as though on angels' wings, by its own power. A God who humbles himself, is condemned, dies, is not the God of the Pure, he is invented by the sinful weakness of those who do not know the truth and cannot be taught it.

This and much besides must be understood if one is to have any kind of idea of the Gnostic movement. Here I have isolated only one basic element from the great variety of Gnostic ideas and systems—an absolute 'gnosis', so to speak, which can develop into whatever system corresponds best to the basic presuppositions of the day; to be more exact, a psychological structure which becomes a 'gnosis' as soon as it takes root in a person's experience. But I see this as an historical realization of those inner strivings of man which I discussed earlier.

In the second century a man opposed these 'pure' and 'enlightened' ones who wanted to banish God to the sunny side of the world. He was born in Asia Minor c. 115, and named Irenaeus—a name that foretold his destiny as a man of peace who until he died a martyr's death was to defend God's almighty power and mercy. Irenaeus became the father of our present faith, which sustains us in the troubles of our daily life. He was a pupil of St Polycarp, who in his turn had received the faith from St John the Evangelist. We know very little of his life. Fate took him from Asia Minor to Gaul. He was probably responsible for bringing Christianity to a great part of Eastern Gaul. As Bishop of Lyons he opposed the Gnostic heresy by preaching and in his writings. We know little more of his life. His writings, *Elenchos kai anatrope tes pseudonomon gnoseos* (literally, the unmasking and defeating of false teaching), more usually known as *Adversus haereses,* consist of five books in Greek, and have been preserved in a faithful Latin translation.

There are important Greek and Armenian fragments, especially from Books 4 and 5. The whole work was completed, with interruptions, between AD 180 and 190. It was supremely important for us and the future of Christianity.

Irenaeus' message was of a good God. Jesus' words from the Gospel of Mark exemplify Irenaeus' basic understanding of the history of mankind : 'The kingdom of God is as if a man should scatter seed upon the ground, and should sleep and rise night and day, and the seed should sprout and grow, he knows not how' (Mark 4.26–7). Irenaeus saw in this a likeness to the story of man, growing towards a goal which is, humanly speaking, unattainable. That goal is divinization. But how does God create gods? Irenaeus must have possessed a very fine mind to have been able to ask that question in the first place, and to press forward thus to the very core of Christ's message: 'We have not been made gods from the beginning, but at first merely men, then at length gods; although God has adopted this course out of his pure benevolence, that no one may impute to him invidiousness or grudgingness. He declares, "I have said, you are gods; and you are all sons of the Highest." ' (*The Writings of Irenaeus* [adapted] vol. 2, pp. 44–5, translated by Alexander Roberts & W. H. Rambaut [Edinburgh, 1868]; IV, 38 : 4.)

How can the divine arise from human existence, which is given over to suffering and death?—'How shall he be a God, who has not as yet been made a man? . . . If, then, you are God's workmanship, await the hand of your Maker which creates everything in due time; in due time as far as you are concerned, whose creation is being carried out. Offer him your heart in a soft and tractable state, and preserve the form in which the Creator has fashioned you, having moisture in yourself lest, by becoming hardened, you lose the impressions of his fingers. But by preserving the framework you will ascend to that which is perfect, for the moist clay which is in you is hidden [there] by the workmanship of God. His hand fashioned your substance. He will cover you over [too] within and without with pure gold and silver, and he will adorn you to such a degree, that even "the King himself will have pleasure in your beauty." But if you, being obstinately hardened, reject the operation of his skill and show yourself ungrateful towards him, because you were created a [mere] man, by becoming thus ungrateful to God, you have at once lost both his workmanship and life. For creation is an attribute of the goodness of God; but to be created is that of human nature.' (*Ibid.*, pp. 46–7; IV 39:2.)

In Irenaeus' view, man (as God conceived him) does not yet exist. *Creation is not yet ended.* It will reach its final perfection only when man enters heaven—the sphere intended for him, This idea of creation Irenaeus drew from the Bible text on how man was created, in God's 'image', after his 'likeness' (*homoiosis*). The history of man is one ascent (today we should say 'evolution') from his original state of being—under God's guidance and forming influence—towards a final point (Teilhard de Chardin would call it the 'Omega point'): to divinization in God: 'By this arrangement, and these harmonies, and a sequence of this nature, man, a created and organized being, is rendered after the image and likeness of the uncreated God—the Father planning everything well and giving his commands, the Son carrying these into execution and performing the work of creating, and the Spirit nourishing and increasing [what is made], but man making progress day by day, and ascending towards the perfect, that is, approximating to the uncreated One. For the Uncreated is perfect, that is, God. Now it was necessary that man should in the first instance be created; and having been created, should receive growth; and having received growth, should be strengthened; and having been strengthened, should abound; and having abounded, should recover [from the disease of sin]; and having recovered, should be glorified; and being glorified, should see his Lord. For God is he who is yet to be seen, and the beholding of God is productive of immortality, but immortality renders one nigh unto God.' (*Ibid.*, p. 44; IV, 38 : 3.)

This actual structure of human development is the aspect of God's creative activity that is turned toward us. It does not mean a forcing of things into a ready-made mould, but an ongoing development of human nature from the womb of being. Man is not yet completed. He is essentially a growing creature, who will only be completed in heaven, by the immediate presence of God.

With these ideas Irenaeus thrust boldly into the outermost danger zones of human thought, to grasp human nature in all its tension. What an adventure of the spirit! This synoptic view or creative synthesis—without any prototype or any support from earlier theology, simply springing from the genius of Irenaeus, in all sincerity, between salvation history and creation, between man's creation, development, often murky history and absolute future—is the unique and decisive achievement in intellectual history of second-century theology, unshakable in its optimism. It was the starting-point of the world-view developed later by Bergson, Blondel and Teilhard de Chardin.

In Irenaeus' understanding of history, there is no division between the reality of the world and the sphere of Christianity. For him the world is in constant transformation. As it rises up towards man it is integrated into God's plan of salvation. Perhaps most important of all, we have here a man who, possibly for the first time, was able to see and experience the world and nature within a Christian concept, who could not separate faith and worldly knowledge, worship and life. A man for whom everything in the world was holy and nothing unholy, who refused to exclude any part of reality from his Christian sympathy, who saw in the world and humanity an object of the infinite love of God, whose joy was in the vitality of his creation.

It requires courage and greatness of soul to think of men in this way, to make way in one's own heart for an all-conquering hope; to be resolved to believe that our world, dark as it often is, and our experience, everything that happens to us and affronts us, are not alien to God; that in the being of the world there is a mysterious meaning, a dynamics that aims at perfection.

But how is the experience of evil to be integrated into such a picture of the world? Our experience bears a double face. On the one hand, evil exists. We experience it above all as suffering and, in its destructive reality, as death. On the other hand, God is the absolute Good. He is creator

of the universe and his love has only one goal, to lead man
into the indestructibility of eternal life. 'Gloria Dei vivens
homo' (the glory of God is a living man; *Ibid.*, I, p. 444;
IV, 20 : 7). Irenaeus gave even human death a comforting
interpretation. In the biblical view, death arose when God
separated man from the tree of everlasting life and drove
him out of Paradise. For Irenaeus this expulsion of man
from Paradise, out of the environment of life and immortality, was not a punishment but an act of mercy by
God towards his fallen creature: 'And God . . . removed
him far from the tree of life . . . because he pitied him,
[and did not desire] that he should continue a sinner
for ever, nor that the sin which surrounded him should be
immortal, and evil interminable and irremediable. But he
set a bound to man's [state of] sin, by interposing death,
and thus causing sin to cease, by putting an end to it by
the dissolution of the flesh, which should take place in
the earth, so that man, ceasing at length to live in sin,
and dying to it, might begin to live to God.' (*Ibid.*, p. 367;
III, 23 : 6.)

This is a unique piece of brilliant theology. It has not
been fully evaluated by even the most modern thinkers of
our faith, let alone further developed. With this idea
Irenaeus created the possibility of a new interpretation of
human death and suffering, an understanding of our
vulnerability as an expression of God's will for our
salvation. Behind this thought, as behind Irenaeus' whole
conception of being, stands the image of a God who is
great, good, and master over all evil: 'Just as God is
always the same, so also man, when found in God, shall
always go on towards God. Neither does God at any time
cease to confer benefits upon, or to enrich man . . . For

the receptacle of his goodness, and the instrument of his glorification, is the man who is grateful to him that made him . . . He [has] promised that he will give very much to those always bringing forth fruit . . . "Well done," he says, "good and faithful servant . . . enter into the joy of the Lord." The Lord himself thus promises very much.' (*Ibid.*, p. 406; IV, 11 : 2.)

This image of God represents a victory for hopeful thinking. In no sphere of his existence, neither in happiness nor in pain, can man withdraw from God's good will toward him: 'For never at any time did Adam escape the hands of God.' (*Ibid.*, vol. II, p. 58; V, 1 : 3.) There are not 'two hands' of God, one which blesses, and the other which punishes. God's touch is always benevolent and creative: '. . . nor another hand of God besides that which, from the beginning even to the end, forms us and prepares us for life, and is present with his handiwork, and perfects it after the image and likeness of God.' (*Ibid.*, p. 99; V, 16 : 1.)

But if human history is the preparation and execution of divinization it must also be so for the vision of God: '. . . revealing God to men through many dispensations, lest man, falling away from God altogether, should cease to exist . . . the life of man consists in beholding God.' (*Ibid.*, vol. I, p. 444; IV, 20 : 7.)

So that man may have room to advance, however, God preserves his invisibility. The fundamental existential straining in man toward an ever-greater God may not be broken—otherwise life's tension would be lost: '. . . preserving at the same time the invisibility of the Father, lest man should at any time despise God, and so that he should always possess something towards which he can advance.' (*Ibid.*)

Hence God reveals his mysteries only bit by bit, leading man step by step into his own life. According to Irenaeus, our knowledge of God also has a history of true advance from imperfect to perfect. All must happen in proper order, neither too early nor too late, in the right relationship to man's capacity to accept and live by it: 'Therefore the Son of the Father declares [the Father] from the beginning . . . in regular order and connexion, at the fitting time for the benefit [of mankind]. For where there is a regular succession, there is also fixedness; and where fixedness, there is suitability to the period; and where suitability, there also utility. And for this reason did the Word become the dispenser of the paternal grace for the benefit of men, for whom he made such great dispensations, revealing God indeed to men.' (*Ibid.*)

But what is this guidance by the good God? Instruction in the knowledge of God, God's ever-increasing revelation, will never end, not even in heaven. Man will always be the one who progresses continually in God, and receives ever more from God. God's immensity cannot be exhausted by any created capacity to receive it. For man, God is always greater. Not only in this world, but in the next, in heaven. Our perfection in the glorified existence of heaven will consist in an ever-growing advance into God, along the dimension of perfection: '. . . there are some things [the knowledge of] which belongs only to God . . . and that not only in the present world, but also in that which is to come, so that God should for ever teach, and man should forever learn the things taught him by God. As the apostle has said on this point, that, when other things have been done away, then these three, "faith, hope and charity, shall endure." For faith, which has respect to our Master, endures unchangeably . . . while we hope ever to be receiving more from God, and to learn from him, because he is good, and possesses boundless riches, a kingdom without end, and instruction that can never be exhausted.' (*Ibid.*, pp. 221–2; II, 28 : 3.)

In my opinion this view of the world, this achievement in thought of a heart inspired by hope, can never be reversed. With Irenaeus a powerful movement of hope broke out in Christian thought. He dragged Christian life from the dead end of despair. He turned his mind to the future, and tore down walls of division set up by pessimism and lack of faith. On such an intellectual basis a life of faith can be built up even in a world of transitory gloom and apparent God-forsakenness. Irenaeus' confidence set men free for greater actions. The transformation of their picture of the world, which first appears with him, was to have decisive and far-reaching consequences for the future of Christendom. It affects the whole man in his understanding of life and the world, because it makes man and the world comprehensible in terms of salvation. But how did Irenaeus acquire his confidence?

It was, I believe, his encounter with Christ that gave him courage and hope with which to interpret the dark history of mankind in the light of God. God appeared among us in the form of a child. For Irenaeus this was an event of symbolic significance. God, who with us became a child, is the ground and origin of our hope. God's becoming a child with us is to be the basis for interpretation of human history for all time: 'The Son of God, although he was perfect, passed through the state of infancy in common with the rest of mankind, sharing it not for his own benefit, but for that of the infantile stage of man's

existence, in order that man might be able to receive him.'
(*Ibid.*, vol. II, p. 43; IV, 38 : 2.) . . . 'It was possible for
God himself to have made man perfect from the first,
but man could not receive that [perfection], being as yet
an infant . . . [God] might easily have come to us in his immortal glory, but in that case we should never have endured the greatness of the glory.' (*Ibid.*, p. 42; IV, 38 : 1.)

God wanted to teach men, 'accustoming man to bear
God's spirit [within him], and to hold communion with
God'. (*Ibid.*, vol. I, p. 417; IV, 14 : 2.) And so Christ
came to us 'that he might gather us into the bosom of the
Father.' (*Ibid.*, vol. II, p. 57; V, 2 : 1.) In Christ 'the
blending and communion of God and man took place
according to the good pleasure of the Father'. (*Ibid.*, vol.
I, p. 441; IV, 20 : 4.)

The Word of God 'dwelt in man, and became the Son of
Man, that he might accustom man to receive God, and
God to dwell in man'. (*Ibid.*, p. 349; III, 20 : 2.) 'For it
was incumbent upon the Mediator between God and men,
by his relationship to both, to bring both to friendship and
concord, and present man to God, while he revealed God
to man.' (*Ibid.*, p. 343; III, 18 : 7.) God also, according to
Irenaeus, had to accustom himself to men: God 'also
descended on the Son of God, made the Son of man,
becoming accustomed in fellowship with him to dwell in
the human race, to rest with human beings, and to dwell
in the workmanship of God'. (*Ibid.*, p. 334; III, 17 : 1.)
With Christ's action in becoming a child with us the age
of transitoriness in our history was closed and our life in
glory begun; 'so that his offspring, the first-begotten Word,
should descend upon the creature, that is, to what had been
moulded, and that it should be contained by him; and,

on the other hand, the creature should contain the Word, and ascend to him, passing beyond the angels, and be made after the image and likeness of God'. (*Ibid.*, vol. II, p. 157; V, 36 : 3.)

One day the eternal Sabbath will arrive. Man will enter into the deep peace of the Godhead and reach his final form of life. The seventh day of creation dawns: 'Upon the seventh day, which has been sanctified, in which God rested from all the works which he created . . . in which they shall not be engaged in any earthly occupation; but shall have a table at hand prepared for them by God, supplying them with all sorts of dishes.' (*Ibid.*, pp. 144–5; V, 33 : 2.) In a sentence, *the universe is a vessel and habitation of the divine Being.*

Christ is the 'heart' of creation. His power is at work at all times and places. This is the response of one who loves. Of a man who has learned to find God everywhere, even in obscure suffering and in the deepest needs of human life. Man suffers, and not only today, from the impression that God is absent. He often sees no connexion between his experience of life and his faith in Christ. Irenaeus says to such a man, in the blessed unconcern of his hope—God is near; he is the infinite precursor and goal of all life in the world. Everything that rises up to God, everything that grows in life, is converging towards its perfection. In this view, a new depth opens up in the massive reality of daily life. The world around us and in us becomes a 'holy place'. God is concentrated within our life, as a drive toward the Infinite. This is the vision of an open world, a universe opened up to eternal perfection, and transformed, in us men, into heaven. We live in a world destined to become transparent to God.

Nietzsche and bewilderment

Nietzsche and bewilderment

Honesty and patience, however, are still far from summing up the attitude with which I, as a thinker, confront reality. Something else is very important: bewilderment. I have been trying lately to go back into my own past, so far as I can. Childhood memories that more and more illuminate the landscape of my being. Even without my wishing it they arise in my soul on all kinds of occasions. At the same time there come the longing to uncover them, look at them, and the marvellous pleasure of telling them to myself anew. They light up, like the sparkling stained-glass windows of Gothic cathedrals, the hard and stony substance of my present existence and turn it into a mystery illumined by points of light.

As long as I can recall, my attitude to the world and to people has been determined by an *almost insuperable indecisiveness*. This mounts up inside me at times to the point of complete confusion. A strange helplessness takes possession of me and expresses itself in the intellectual field as an element of 'both . . . and' in my searchings as a thinker. Only too often I am prostrated by the experience of how separate and opposed realities co-exist in our life, and are indissolubly bound together—love and hate, joy and sorrow, blessings and curses, life and death, decision-making and uncertainty, and others too. I have always looked at the various events of my life in this context.

I was basically familiar with Luther's great 'both . . .

and' : *both just and sinner.* Together with this experience there entered into my life a great loneliness in face of a world ever more alienating and yet constantly drawing closer. It is true that today I can master all these contradictions without any logical objection by applying the principle of analogy, the teaching that in every likeness there arises a still greater unlikeness. But I cannot do so in the existential field where conclusive thinking is done—in the heart.

At that level the insoluble problems remain and have to be endured and survived in ever greater acts of mastery. Why did I want to start out at all in the field of intellectual inquiry with such a disposition—such an unfortunate one, many would say? Today I must honestly admit to myself— for no reason, absolutely none! On the one hand I never wanted to 'improve' the world, or to instruct others. On the other there was never, since my beginnings as a thinker, any 'in order to', only a strange 'having to think', connected, perhaps, with curiosity about how much truth a man can bear.

There was no question with me—apart from certain isolated lamentable attempts—of a system of truth, perhaps not even of 'the truth' at all, but of something fundamentally different : being and remaining truthful, the essential truths of my own life. Only now has it become clear to me how much individualization, subjectivity and danger to one's own existence and that of others such an attitude to thinking bears within itself.

I must also admit that these experiences—both the prostration and the search for the true basis of my own life— are not merely narrow, but narrowing perspectives. Yet they led me to other people, to the masters of thought, in an attitude of readiness for encounter and seeking for advice, in inner need. Therefore my thought arose from encounter. Curiously a text from Nietzsche was of decisive importance to me in this search for counsel: 'I teach you the Superman. Man is something that should be overcome. What have you done to overcome him? . . . The Superman is the meaning of the earth. Let your will say: The Superman *shall be* the meaning of the earth. I entreat you, my brothers, *remain true to the earth* . . .' (*Thus Spake Zarathustra*, translated by R. J. Hollingdale [London, 1961], pp. 41–2.)

That was Friedrich Nietzsche's challenging cry, in his perhaps most important work. I had always been very careful to assess these sentences of Nietzsche's correctly. Many Christians, including Pierre Teilhard de Chardin, have spoken penetratingly and in a Christian sense of a 'superman'. Nor was I impressed by the fact that the Nazi ideology adopted this idea in a superficial way. Nietzsche had nothing to do with that. I am trying to enter more deeply into Nietzsche's mental world and to get to grips with his philosophical attitude. Seldom has a thinker philosophized so personally as he did. IIis strongly subjective assertions and predictions remind me of the prophets and founders of religions.

I know just how heavily burdened Nietzsche was in a human sense, but you can't reproach him for that. Nietzsche lost his father before he was five. He grew up in a domestic world dominated exclusively by women: his grandmother, two aunts, his young mother and his sister were the guiding forces. Nietzsche's home was a stronghold of Protestant piety, adhering for generations to the Lutheran faith: God-fearing, righteous and provincial. It incorporated all the virtues and convictions of German Protestant clericalism. I do not want to reproduce Nietzsche's life in detail. It is well-known or can easily be read in good biographies.

I want to mention only his close connexion with Switzerland. In February 1869 came the official call to Basle even before he had obtained his doctorate. He was then twenty-five. A year later his special professorship was transformed into a regular chair of classical philology. Nietzsche had attained in his mid-twenties nearly everything worth striving for in the course of an academic career: he was a young scholar whose words and judgments were taken seriously; he had good pupils, to whom he was a tolerably good teacher; he had reached the professor's chair earlier than others, and with it the highest levels of his career; he could lead a largely independent life and had real friends.

Ten years later he gave up the professorship in Basle and soon moved to Sils-Maria. He lived alone, and apart. There, in the Upper Engadine, he felt for the first time some relief: 'Perhaps St Moritz is really the right place. For me it is as if I were in the land of promise . . . For the first time feelings of relief . . . It does me good. I will stay a long time here.'

He was seized by a strange exaltation, which was however subject to sharp changes. Still, he was happy in Sils-Maria in a way he had not known before. He discovered the first ideas for his *Zarathustra*. We do not know what released this euphoria of Nietzsche's which set in here for the first time. Perhaps his condition improved a little, or perhaps his illness altered. Certainly the magic of Sils played a part in this exaltation. He lived as a recluse, in a back room in a small house set a little apart from the street, by the woods, shady and protected from the bright light that his eyes could so ill endure.

Here he led the life of a thinker: quiet, walking by the lake and in the mountain forest, following his thoughts, reading hard and writing, secluded and withdrawn. There took shape the image, so often described, of the lonely Nietzsche. All these circumstances combined to create a strange mood: 'Thoughts have risen up on my horizon the like of which I have never seen . . . I really must live for some years yet.' He was indeed to live another twenty years, half of them however in mental derangement, cared for by his mother and, after her death, his sister.

On 3 January 1889 he had a nervous collapse, on the Piazza Carlo Alberto in Turin. A few days later a friend fetched him and took him, a sick man, to the nerve clinic in Basle. The diagnosis at Basle was general paralysis of the insane. In the middle of January his mother took him away to Jena, where Nietzsche was admitted to Professor Binswanger's clinic. Nietzsche's derangement lasted more than a decade. After his mother's death in 1897 his sister took care of him. She moved with Nietzsche into a house in Weimar where she not only looked after her mentally-ill brother but also assembled his books, manuscripts and notes. Soon a Nietzsche cult arose, of which however he himself knew nothing. He died on 25 August 1900 and was buried in the cemetery at Röcken, next to his father.

I have had to leave out many details in this short portrayal. Above all, his many-sided, in part tragic, friendships are very important in elucidating Nietzsche's life. Nor have I mentioned the various journeys, above all in Italy. Instead I should like to give an interpretation of some of the fourth part of Nietzsche's most important book: *Thus Spake Zarathustra*: Part IV, The Sorcerer.

Of course it is asking too much to take this relatively

short text as a basis for interpreting Nietzsche's work. My excuse consists simply in the fact that I do not wish to interpret Nietzsche's work, but only to show what influence this particular text had on the development of my thinking.

The whole book arose in four stages. Nietzsche wrote the first three parts in the course of a year. They were written with startling suddenness of inspiration. The actual writing of each part can be reckoned as scarcely more than ten days: first part, February 1883 in Rapallo; second part, June 1883 in Sils-Maria; third part, January 1884 in Nice. The fourth part is markedly different from those preceding it. It was written, with interruptions, between autumn 1884 and February 1885. The passage with which I am concerned begins with a story.

Zarathustra is walking alone in the mountains. Looking over a rock he sees a man, not far beneath him, lying on the ground. As Nietzsche puts it: 'But when he ran to the spot where the man lay on the ground, he found a trembling old man with staring eyes; and however much Zarathustra tried to raise him and set him upon his legs, it was in vain. Neither did the unfortunate man seem to notice that there was anyone with him; on the contrary, he continually looked around him with pathetic gestures, like one forsaken by and isolated from all the world. Eventually, however, after much trembling, quivering, and self-contortion, he began to wail thus.' (pp. 264–5.)

Here Nietzsche sketches the basic situation of human life. Man is *abandoned and alone*. This apparent situation draws from him speech that basically is not speech at all but wailing. The expression 'wail' is here used for speech, since the man is not certain whether anyone is listening (perhaps this points to the reality that Karl Rahner applies to prayer

—'words into silence'). How does this wailing go?

> Who still warms me, who still loves me?
> Offer me hot hands!
> Offer me coal-warmers for the heart!
> Spread-eagled, shuddering,
> Like a half-dead man whose feet are warmed—
> Shaken, alas! by unknown fevers,
> Trembling with sharp icy frost-arrows,
> Pursued by you, my thought!
> Unutterable, veiled, terrible one!
> Huntsman behind the clouds!
> Struck down by your lightning-bolt,
> You mocking eye that stares at me from the darkness
>   —thus I lie,
> Bend myself, twist myself, tortured
> By every eternal torment,
> smitten
> By you, cruel huntsman,
> You unknown—God! (p. 265.)

A highly significant beginning. Human existence in the world is conditioned by an experience of God. The account begins with 'longing':

> Who still warms me, who still loves me?
> Offer me hot hands!
> Offer me coal-warmers for the heart! (p. 265.)

The outcome of reflexion begins here at the same level as with Augustine or Blondel. But 'who still warms me' is a profound cry from the depths of the creature. This cry is uncontrollable, it springs from an essential human drive. To be warmed : that is a vital need for the living creature. The longing for warming, for a womb, for someone to be close to in the chill of our world. No one can escape this longing—to spiritualize it and lift it to a higher plane is possible, but not fundamentally to escape it.

The 'spirit-bearing body' is stretched out, stricken by frosty arrows. The man is pursued by his anxiety—this is the reverse side of our longing, 'rejection'. What sort of life is that? Man is delivered over to the cold—at once fully alive and half dead. He is shaken by fears and needs, but also by intimations. He is pursued by his thought. This means, he is torn away from the living, warm nearness of the blood, from the animal warmth of life without consciousness. He needs his feet warmed, this spirit-bearing body. What causes this monstrous tension in human existence? Nietzsche tries to find out.

It is something which he characterizes first in four ways : it is the 'unutterable, veiled, terrible one'. Anyone who has some acquaintance with the Greek Fathers will know at once who is meant by this first description : it is God. We cannot prettify God.

For us he is unutterable, veiled, and sometimes also terrible. His mystery is eternally impenetrable. That is the reason for our torment on earth, but also for our eternal happiness in heaven. He remains the eternally unknown God. That is why in heaven too we can advance eternally further into him, receive more from him, as Irenaeus has told us. He remains hidden from us in the very act of revealing himself. Of course, the difference between our life on earth and in heaven is that here God is sometimes truly terrible (in his grandeur, greatness, demands and power); there—however we picture heaven to ourselves

—his obscurity and hiddenness become a constantly growing happiness for us.

His second name is 'huntsman'. He will not grant any
man rest. Why? I believe it is because he is the God of
my life. He wants to say something more than ordinarily
personal, and also to demand it from me. I have to find
out who this God is, the God I experience in my life beyond
formulations, concepts and systems. The Christian message,
precisely because of its positive demand for a truly human
existence in the sight of God, is an impassioned protest
against human falsity. It is thus a protest against the false
piety of the letter which lacks the experience of God, and
protest against all religious activity that does not correspond
to the inner reality of the heart. Here man is addressed and
challenged by God in his whole existence. Therefore he
is the 'huntsman'.

Nietzsche's third description of God is as 'eye'. This is
a profound symbol of biblical spirituality. In this connexion 'eye' means that God watches me constantly, that
nothing in me escapes him, that he observes me, that
nothing in me can be strange to him. Man is delivered
up into God's knowledge, even in his most secret wishes and
thoughts. To know this, to live accordingly and affirm it,
can be the highest stage of sanctity. To be afraid of it
means that, as Nietzsche puts it, the eye of God is
'mocking'.

Finally, the fourth description of God: one who is in
'darkness'. God looks upon us from out of the darkness,
out of a realm that we can never explore completely. I must
be quite honest with myself: is this not also my experience
of God, or should it be so? In any case the fathers of the
Church repeatedly experienced God as darkness. This is

perhaps the most distinctive and existentially most significant of the 'names of God'. God lives 'behind the clouds'. This was also the experience of Moses, who for the first time, and most powerfully, 'brought down' God to us. And this is the experience of all of us: God comes towards me from out of the darkness. To affirm this darkness, to submit oneself to it, can heal my life from within, give it strength and courage.

Nietzsche's account goes on:

> Strike deeper!
> Strike once again!
> Sting and sting, shatter this heart!
> What means this torment
> With blunt arrows? (p. 265.)

The special characteristic of God's 'torment' is that it does not represent an absolute. It is not massive, mortal, but is inflicted with 'blunt arrows'. God could bring all that to an end. But he does not do it, he does not strike deeply enough. This is God's curious psychology with us. He lets us, if we can express it so—'stew in our own juice'. He does not break our heart but torments us by giving us no peace. Occasionally he is in a hurry. Usually, however, he gives himself plenty of time. A man has to get used to this, to sense the time of grace. Unfortunately man often does not give himself as much time as God himself grants him.

Man thinks he must manage everything at once. I see something very wrong in this: why cannot a man put off a problem for a time, even a decision of faith? Even when it is a matter of vital truths of faith. Why do we not give ourselves more time? Perhaps the moment has not yet come to believe everything at once. God gives us time. I believe it is quite possible that he does not demand everything from us at once, that it is acceptable to put some matters aside. It is of course understood that this is not to deny them, but to say: I have not yet received the grace for that. I am giving myself the chance to mature, to reach understanding.

I must therefore realize that God has much time and does not demand everything at once. In the Christian life faith takes effect at various times. Sometimes one truth enlightens me, sometimes another. We should regard our life as a unity. This great unity is what matters. If God himself 'will not strike deep enough', then we should have *patience with ourselves*. This is an essential precondition of sanctity. Not unbelief, but the road to our sanctification. The rest of this passage can be understood from that starting-point:

> Why do you look down,
> Unwearied of human pain,
> With malicious divine flashing eyes?
> Will you not kill,
> Only torment, torment?
> Why—torment *me*,
> You malicious, unknown God?
>
> Ha ha! Are you stealing near?
> At such a midnight hour
> What do you want? Speak!
> You oppress me, press me—
> Ha! far too closely!
> Away! Away!
> You hear me breathing,

> You overhear my heart,
> You jealous God—
> Yet, jealous of what?
> Away! Away! Why the ladder? (pp. 265–6.)

God's being is revealed. He is a jealous God. This is again a biblical description of God. What is he jealous of, and why? He will not tolerate any other God beside himself. God is everything that our heart demands, totally. God is much too close to us. He has a 'ladder' by which he climbs directly into our heart. These images mean that God is near to us in a completely personal way. He is neither an image nor a concept, but a person. Only a person can be jealous. We see how for Nietzsche the idea of God grows with each step in his thought. In his head he may have been an atheist, but in his heart he was certainly a Christian. The next verse shows this :

> Would you climb
> Into my heart,
> Climb into my most secret
> Thoughts?
> Shameless, unknown—thief!
> What would you get by stealing?
> What would you get by listening?
> What would you get by torturing,
> You torturer?
> You—Hangman-god! (p. 266.)

Once again biblical concepts loom up. First, the 'heart'. That is the image for the 'thou', for its uniqueness, indeed for the uniqueness of the unique. It is the 'place' where the concrete reality of man, his body and soul, his wishes and thoughts are bound together in an indissoluble unity. God wants to climb down into this uniqueness. And only he can do this. He creeps in—he is the 'thief'. This passage could just as well come from the Bible, perhaps the book of Job. I see no blasphemy in it, but the outcry of a tormented and honest heart. And whose heart is not tormented?

Or shall I like a dog,
Roll before you?
Surrendering, raving with rapture,
Wag—love to you?

In vain! Strike again,
Cruellest knife! No,
Not dog—I am only your game,
Cruellest huntsman!
Your proudest prisoner,
You robber behind the clouds!
For the last time, speak!

What do you want, waylayer, from me?
You God veiled in lightning! Unknown One!
Speak,
What do you want, unknown—God? (p. 266.)

If a man deals with God in such a way, with such existential abandon, then he is no 'dog' before God. God doesn't want a man to roll before him like a dog. God doesn't want to make him tame—and won't tame him. He is no dog in God's sight but his 'game', his 'proudest prisoner'. We have not yet fully grasped that man is the image and likeness of God.

I want to mention only the *freedom of man*. Man is free, but what does freedom mean? Either one is free,

or one is not. The difference consists only in how often
one exercises this capacity to be free. In the last analysis
God is not 'more free' than man. If man gives himself to
God, this happens in the utmost freedom, or there is no
gift, and no friendship either. For the heart of another free
being one must do battle. Even God cannot suspend this
basic law of life. Friendship does not arise from cringing,
but is often born out of hard struggle. Of course God can
and must remain the victor. He is a 'waylayer' and a 'huntsman'. If we neglect this aspect of our relationship with God
then we have only a small and petty God, who does not
exist.

> What? Ransom?
> How much ransom?
> Demand much—thus speaks my pride!
> And be brief—thus speaks my other pride!
> *Me*—you want me?
> Me—all of me? . . . (pp. 266-7.)

Clearly God wants no 'ransom'. He will neither ask
much nor speak long. He would like to have from man
something fundamentally different: the man himself—
the whole of him. The concept of 'redemption' is here
fundamentally inverted by Nietzsche. God needs nothing
from man, no external contribution, no paying-off of a
debt. He does not speak with human pride. He would
much prefer to have the man himself, the whole man. But
that is at the level where nothing can be forced. That is
the level of friendship. If we want to understand the full
range of his thought then we must rely on our human
experience, reflect on what can happen in human inclination, and again what God's friendship can create in us.

In human friendship I perhaps receive nothing definable of my 'thou'. I receive the gift of being able to say to a man, 'thou'. Before that, before this friendship, I was no 'I'. I was only the part I played, indeed had to play. But since I have had a 'thou', I have become an 'I'. The two of us, by being together, are a 'we'. In friendship the being of the other becomes my own. We are together. The course of human friendship is an image of what is meant by salvation. To be with God in friendship is to live in an exchange of being with him. The being of God becomes our own. From this there follows something I almost dare not express: I have become God. I have become a son of the Father, because Christ is Son of the Father. My love of God is the same with which Christ himself loves the Father—the Holy Spirit.

I cannot penetrate this mystery of salvation, of my life in the triune God. A dizzying abyss opens there. Into this depth, this mystery of the inner life of God in which God is God, the Father in the Son, the Son in the Father, and both one in the love of the Holy Spirit, I am drawn also. I must try here to forget words, even words like 'immortality', 'resurrection', 'last judgment' and 'purgatory', perhaps the very word 'heaven' itself. I must try to allow the reality of salvation, which I can here express only haltingly, to enter more closely into my heart.

> Ha ha!
> And you torment me, fool that you are,
> You rack my pride?
> Offer me love—who still warms me?
> Who still loves me?—offer me hot hands!
> Offer me coal-warmers for the heart,

C

Offer me, the most solitary,
Whom ice, alas! sevenfold ice
Has taught to long for enemies,
For enemies themselves,
Offer, yes yield to me,
Cruellest enemy—
Yourself!

He is gone!
He himself has fled,
My last, sole companion,
My great enemy,
My unknown,
My Hangman-god! (p. 267.)

The theme of flight is sounded here—another biblical
idea. Evidently man cannot endure the nearness of God.
He flees from God, as the prophet Jonah once fled from
his mission in God's sight. But I cannot help knowing
that it is not easy to endure God's full demand. He can
appear to us as an enemy, unknown, as the hangman-God.
Perhaps Nietzsche was broken against this God. And not
only Nietzsche! I can see that even Jesus himself could
not endure the constant presence of the Father. Jesus'
life was no grandiose 'drama'. In the Garden of Olives,
he threw himself to the ground, cried out, wandered
around, sweated blood. Three times he prayed to the
Father, always saying the same thing—that he could go
on no longer. He stared with wild eyes at the figure of the
angel, who sought to comfort him. In the end he produced a Yes only as a secondary statement, with a fearful
No added to it. Finally he could bear it no longer and
cried out 'It is enough' (Mark 14.4).

That was the mystery of the powerlessness of Jesus, the powerlessness of all the compassionate who want to bear the life of others with them. In a sense that we can never fully comprehend, he descended in his suffering into hell, into the destruction of all hopes. This he endured and thus proved that he was God himself. He threw himself down on the sin-spattered earth, 'burrowed into it', and pressed it to himself. From then on man can and may be sad and full of desperation, even 'God-forsaken'. But he is no longer alone. God is with him. There is no power in the world that can take such a Saviour from us. Those who have made self-seeking and pitiless self-assertion into a rule of life may cause us suffering and want. But in the depths of our being they no longer have power over us. Christ has spoken his eternal Yes to all that is honestly meant in the human heart, to all mildness and forgiveness, to all kindness and hope.

No! Come back,
With all your torments!
Oh come back
To the last of all solitaries!
All the streams of my tears
Run their course to you!
And the last flame of my heart—
It burns up to *you*.
Oh come back,
My unknown God! My pain! My last—happiness!

(p. 267.)

That is the end of this strange declaration. Despite everything, despite rejection and resistance, the man says Yes and calls 'Come back!' All the streams of man's tears

flow into the unknown, to God. The last flame of the
heart glows for him. It is true God is still his pain. But
beyond this he already senses that God is his ultimate
happiness. Is it possible to experience God simultaneously
as happiness and pain? To establish this I must apply two
sequences of thought.

First, the christological basis. Christ lived in the 'vision
of the Father'. There are theologians who assert that this
vision was a 'beatific' one. I believe however that this view
is fundamentally false. How then could one explain
Christ's loneliness and God-forsakenness, his agony and
bloody sweat? Precisely because Christ saw the Father, felt
his closeness, and at the same time was compelled to feel
that he was delivered up to the pain and want, the dis-
order of our world, his suffering became so real, so immeasurable. To live out God's nearness with all the fibres
of his being and at the same time to be exposed to want,
there can only be a very weak image for it—that of
'hell'. It was the vision of the Father that raised Christ's
suffering to immeasurable heights. It was therefore no
'beatific vision' of the Father, but an agonizing vision,
intensifying his suffering, that Christ experienced. He felt
totally in the presence of God, and at the same time
radically separated from him. He longed for the Father
and at the same time knew that the way to him lay through
pain and want. Anyone who has not thought out these
circumstances and their full consequences has really
understood little of the life of Jesus.

Secondly, our own life, too, remains incomprehensible
if we do not reflect on what we are accustomed to term
'eschatological yearning'. It is significant that at the end of
the New Testament there is a full cry of pain and

longing: 'Amen. Come, Lord Jesus!' (Revelation 22.20). In our longing we all live ahead of ourselves. The longing for Christ's return is only the final crystallization of many hopes and yearnings. Only when man reaches out for something unattainable by human power—to call it by its true name, for God—does there arise in him any awareness, knowledge, and will. The challenge must really be so great, so unattainable, if the reality is to supply at least a small part of what, fundamentally, is laid upon it. Without yearning human awareness becomes stunted; and absence of longing for Christ's return stunts Christian life itself.

Here I should like to introduce another question. Can a person, and above all can a Christian, still feel joy in such a situation? Certainly, our message to the world is *good news*. In this sense we should all write our 'good news', perhaps not with ink and paper, but with our own lives. To *be* joy, not simply to *have* joy, is not just a good quality, not merely a little cheerfulness, a happy feeling in oneself. For us it is a Christian duty—sometimes even a very heavy duty in daily life. But how can this be? To be honest, I don't really know. Rather than discuss the question at length I should like to take a small example from the *Little Flowers of St Francis*: 'At last Brother Leo spoke up and said, "Father, I beg you in God's name, tell me where perfect joy is?" Francis replied, "If we were now coming to Santa Maria degli Angeli quite soaked through, chilled all over by rain and cold, and if we then rang at the door and the porter came and said—Who are you? and if when we answered, We are two of your brothers, he brought us closer and said—What? You are two vagabonds who wander about the world taking alms away from the Poor! And he would not open for us, but left us standing outside in snow, wet, frost and hunger until after nightfall . . . And if, after such bad treatment we knocked again, and begged him insistently, with tears, to open to us, and he became enraged and came out with a club and struck us on the cowl, and so beat us that we fell in the mud and snow . . . if we bore all this injustice, injury and beating with the thought that we were bearing the suffering of Christ in all patience . . . Brother Leo, write that *there* lies perfect joy!" ' I do not know whether I myself could gather up enough courage to live like that. It would be glorious!

The story from *Zarathustra* ends strangely. In the end everything remains in suspense. Zarathustra accuses the old man (now called 'the Sorcerer') of being a liar and seducer who wants to test him: 'The old sorcerer was silent for a time, then he said: "Did I test you? I—only seek. O Zarathustra, I seek a genuine man, a proper, simple man, a man of one meaning and of all honesty, a repository of wisdom, a saint of knowledge, a great man!" ' (p. 270.)

As a Christian I am profoundly grateful to Nietzsche (whom Thérèse of Lisieux called her 'little sick brother') for this story.

Erasmus and the centre

Erasmus and the centre

Just as the whole of human existence is founded on an inward, deep centre (or unfolds from it), so there is a centre in every true thought, even though it is often difficult to see it. In the individual man you can sense something of the centre of his being once you have made sure how intensely he responds to given values, such as honour, friendship, love, honesty, and so on. But how does he master the varied events of his own life? From what depth and basis does he create its meaning? What can he affirm totally, with his whole being, and what reject? In what can he be completely absorbed? For what does he accept renunciation, failure or contempt—perhaps even death? Such questions decide for us the nature of the deep-rooted centre of being, widely varying in each individual. Man really lives in this centre. His essential being, his 'heart', the essence of the individual man, is concentrated there.

This centre of being contains ideas also, or at least the seeds of ideas. Of course it is all still unsystematic, interwoven with will, longing, feelings, speculation, joy and fear. Once this thinking centre of the man is set in motion, it releases wave upon wave of more or less connected thoughts. Unexpected riches flow from the centre. In the biblical image of man, men's thoughts spring from the heart. This is why it is so important for me to sense this ultimate, vital centre of thought in the individual thinker, to investigate it with respect and restraint, not as a confrontation or discussion, but in friendly understanding. There are always surprises in meeting such thinkers. Our former world of thought can be entirely transformed by them, or shattered, so that we have to put it together again piece by piece.

That kind of encounter is also shattering because such thinkers belong completely to a powerful uprising of the spirit. With all the indignation their souls can muster, they attack the 'debasement of being' in its many different forms. This is why these people are the great hope of oppressed humanity. Their appearance is always a time of grace for us. They may often not break through at the level of worldly power. But no one can subsequently extinguish their influence. The thinking of the open spirit is superficially enclosed in an oppressive helplessness. The sadness of this situation is familiar to anyone who knows Western thought.

An encounter with the thinking centre of such people can change our whole style of thought. Suddenly something new flows through the veins of our thought, like warm blood, and fills us with a powerful, perhaps hitherto unknown feeling. At such a moment I began to live as a thinker. Real existence, the life of the spirit, set in. It was the moment of my *intellectual birth*.

Not in the sense that it separates me from the earth. The thoughts that well up from a centre of being are completely of the earth, bound up with the universe, very often 'pious' in a simple kind of way. The essential task of the great teachers of thought is to throw themselves totally into the love of wisdom. But wisdom means morally correct recognition, as a result of which a man bases each and every thing as a whole on the reality of God and gives his insights even more validity as moral and religious decisions in actual life.

A thought occurs to me in this connexion that will perhaps disconcert some of my friends. In Dostoievsky's novel *The Brothers Karamazov* the revered Father Zossima solemnly proclaims to the 'people of God', in inspired words, that they should strike roots in a new inwardness, which he calls the 'earth', but which could just as well be rendered as 'centre of being' : 'Fall to the earth and kiss it, sprinkle it with your tears, and the earth will bring you fruit from your tears. Love the earth, love insatiably, love everyone and everything, seek out the exaltation and ecstasy of love. Sprinkle the earth with tears of joy and love those tears of yours.'

The demand to 'kiss the earth' perhaps sounds too emotional and alien to the language of thought. But in my version—'earth' as 'centre of being'—it is only a symbol of what should come 'from the centre' in all thought. I think that anyone who has not yet 'kissed the earth' as a sign of obeisance to an inner reality may well go astray, perhaps in all his thinking.

Erasmus of Rotterdam is relevant here. It is not easy to be just to him. For us today he is at once known and unknown. His fate was scarcely different in his own lifetime. Perhaps that is characteristic of every great man. I wonder who this man really was who still fascinates us five hundred years after his birth—yet whom few really know. Erasmus' personality was very complex. He lived on the border. His life and spirit cannot be easily grasped and described.

The only facts that can be established about his early youth are that he was born the son of a priest and a doctor's daughter, on 28 November 1469 (some say 1466), probably in Rotterdam, and that he had lost his parents by the time he was fourteen. All this (which he later felt to be a stigma) and the lack of home and family, perhaps explain the aspects of his temperament that he found so trying: restlessness, distrust, evasiveness, anxiety to establish himself, sensitivity and need for approval. On top of his illegitimate birth there was a second impediment to his development in mind and character—his weak physical constitution.

All his life he had to contend with illness. He suffered in a harsh climate; couldn't endure heavy wines; and was plagued by gallstones and other complaints. He was small and delicate. One physical defect always caused him particular trouble—the abnormal flatness of the back of his head. In his own caricatures he made fun of this. On account of it he always wore a cap which completely covered the back of his head.

His school education in Deventer was marked by the so-called *devotio moderna*. This was a movement of religious renewal, aiming mainly at a personal, inward piety. The Deventer circle was for a long time the focus of this movement. The 'devout' were concerned above all with a deeply held Christian piety. They set particular store by Scripture reading, and an outlook nourished by it. They were not enthusiastic about scholasticism, but didn't actually oppose it. Their influence on the new forms of piety, particularly on Ignatius of Loyola and his 'exercises', was very marked. The *devotio moderna*, the 'new form of devout life', taught people to turn totally inward and played a large part among those who sought the 'kingdom within'.

When his education was completed, less out of inclination than under pressure of circumstances, Erasmus entered the monastery of Steyn near Gouda. Here, in 1492, he was ordained to the priesthood. Later on, Erasmus did not like to speak of how deeply he had been formed by Deventer and by Steyn. And yet there lived on in him the imperishable fruits of the *devotio moderna*: a piety based on the Bible and the Fathers, a spirituality that looked on the world with concern and mistrust, a critical attitude to all the outward forms of the Church and to the clergy, an inward concept of worship and the sacraments, and above all an almost childlike tender piety towards Christ.

Erasmus succeeded, without great difficulty, in moving from Steyn to the service of the bishop of Cambrai. This happened directly after his ordination. The bishop was to have taken him as a companion on his journey to Italy, but cancelled the trip for as yet unknown reasons. We know that in 1495 the bishop sent Erasmus to Paris. Erasmus entered the Collège Montaigu, first as a student, then as a tutor. Apparently he was never happy in Paris. But despite the unpleasant things he wrote about the Collège Montaigu he spoke of Aquinas only with deep respect.

Only of England can it be said that it became a 'homeland' for him. There he put down roots and flowered. He also discovered his life's work there. During his first visit to England in the years 1499–1500, he met with such men as John Colet, a Christian humanist, and with his theology founded on the Bible and the Fathers of the Church. In 1504 he wrote him a letter which expressed many of his most private plans: 'I am now making full tilt for the books of the Bible . . . For three years now only the Greek has counted for me . . . I have read nearly all Origen's works and it seems to me that thanks to his guidance I have already achieved something . . . In no literature can we understand anything without Greek, for supposing is not the same as judging; to see with one's own eyes is different from trusting to those of others.'

At about the same time he began a friendship with Thomas More. The correspondence between Erasmus and More was not only extensive, and continued almost up to More's death, but supplies much evidence of their unclouded mutual relationship. Without doubt Erasmus felt profoundly the force of More's personality. The equanimity of his nature, and its truly wise gaiety, qualities that all too often eluded Erasmus, drew him irresistibly to More. At the beginning of his third stay in England (1509–14) Erasmus was to write, in More's house, the famous *Encomium Moriae* (*Praise of Folly*). If you want to know what a humanist was in Erasmus' sense, read his biography of More. It is still the best in existence, written in 1519, when no one could yet know that More would incarnate the *philosophia Christi* in the full sense of the word, by sacrificing his own life.

Erasmus spent the rest of his life mainly in various journeys and intensive intellectual work. We find him for three years in Italy (1506–9), and four more times in England. Between times he spent a short time in Antwerp, Louvain, Cologne, and was repeatedly in Basle. His life there was interrupted only by a few years in Freiburg im Breisgau, in Germany. At the end of his life he returned once more to Basle and died there in 1536.

This short summary naturally tells us little of the intensity and variety of his experiences in all these places. Certainly Italy was almost as important to him as England, though in Erasmus' life there was no 'Italian experience', such as there was for Dürer. Erasmus was not really at home in states and fatherlands but, strange as it may sound, *in the Church*. It was because he loved it that he criticized it so bitterly.

The details of his wandering life can be read in several good accounts. They need not specially detain us here. On the other hand it seems to me important to draw attention to certain major works of Erasmus, from which I should like eventually to distil the character of his mind. I want to divide his works into three periods, rather artificially, but corresponding essentially to the course of his mental development. The division is not intended chronologically, but instead corresponds to concentric circles in his work. In the first circle I find those writings that seek to frame a new 'humanist attitude'.

Humanistic writings: Erasmus depicts the basic attitude of a true Christian humanist as follows: friendly, even festive manners, a cheerful spirit, simplicity in food and manner of life, freedom from rigid formality, a gift for friendship and conversation, joy in the variety of creation, in nature, in the animals, joy in knowledge and many-sided culture, harmony in family life, reserve in the service of the court, seriousness in piety. Among these works I count such various books, so widely separated in time, as *Against the Barbarians* (*Antibarbari*), *Proverbs* (*Adagia*); the *Handbook of the Christian Knight* (*Enchiridion militis christiani*), *Colloquies* (*Colloquia*), the *Praise of Folly* (*Encomium Moriae*); the *Instruction of a Christian*

Prince (*Institutio principis christiani*), and the *Complaint of Peace* (*Quaerela pacis*). As can be seen at once, the period in which these books were produced extended over twenty years, from 1500 to 1520. We are dealing not so much with a chronological period as with a collection of creative works.

Biblical work and patristic texts: In 1516 Erasmus published an edition of the New Testament with notes, and his own Latin translation, departing from the Vulgate, the *Novum Instrumentum*. He made notes for this (*Paraclesis, Methodus* and *Apologia*), a biblical theology, the so-called *Philosophia Christi*. Step by step he commented on various texts of the New Testament: the Letter to the Romans (1517), the rest of the Epistles (1517–21), the Gospels (from 1522) and the Acts of the Apostles (1524).

Alongside this work he was engaged in patristic studies, again out of the deeply felt call for a 'return to the sources': i.e., Cyprian (1521), Arnobius (1522), Hilarius (1523), Irenaeus (1526), Chrysotom (1530). With this opening up of the sources, Erasmus fulfilled the longing of humanist theology, its call of 'back to the sources', and its wish to draw from the original sources of faith, freed from later distortions.

The letters: Some smaller works should also be mentioned: for example, the little book *Free Will* (*De libero arbitrio*, 1524), in which he came out decisively against Luther, or his *Ciceronianus* (1528), in which he disclaimed a humanism for which Cicero meant more than Christ himself.

More than three thousand letters of Erasmus are also known to us, some of them minor masterpieces of discussion. In these letters the happiness and tragedy of his friendships are revealed. Without them it would not be possible to paint a true picture of Erasmus. I have drawn, for my own interpretation, upon important parts of this extensive correspondence.

I should now like, after this almost unworthily brief portrayal of the life and work of Erasmus, to work out the basic ideas in his creative activity. If I am right there are three of these, which are very closely interwoven with each other. I shall consider each separately, and then look at them as a unity.

The idea of humanism: What fascinates me about Erasmus is his purposeful recommendation of a Christian humanism. Even early on I noticed this tendency in him, the effect of the ideal of 'humanitas', of culture according to the model of the ancients. His unconditional commitment to the search for culture alienated him from the life of the cloister and led to an almost permanent conflict with his environment. The monastery seemed to him a stronghold of barbarism. When he wrote *Antibarbari*, which was published only ten years later (and then incompletely), he castigated the monks' hostility to learning.

Erasmus wanted above all to lay the bases of a *philosophia christiana*, a Christian moral philosophy built on the Bible and the Fathers of the Church; more precisely a 'Christian existentialism'. He regarded it as his life's work to open up the Bible to Christians. His edition of the New Testament was an important departure in its time. The proposals Erasmus put forward in his introductions, his call to the laity to make the words and spirit of Holy Scripture their own, can be addressed no less to men of today than to those of his own time. For him, culture was never an end in itself. He had little time for a pagan *humanitas*. Instead he joined antiquity to Christendom in a single unity. In this sense he could revere Socrates, even hail him as 'holy Socrates'. His attitude to antiquity was not historical, but ethical. It offered him *exempla*, examples of the right way of living, as important to know as examples of the Christian life. Therefore I emphasize the primary element of his humanism, the cry of:

Back to the sources. Erasmus' concept of the Church is an intellectual structure of the highest interest. If you look at it more closely, you see central areas of his thought. Fundamental for him was the distinction between a pre-existing Church which has been mysteriously 'present' since the creation of the world, and a new Church that begins with Christ's incarnation, and then a third Church, springing from the Apostles' pentecostal mission and the spreading of the Church over the world.

Here Erasmus took up a very ancient idea on which he based the notion of an invisible Church. An old element in this idea was the belief that behind the Old Testament, long before Christ's birth, there were individual men of such clear spirit that one must regard them as members of the Church. But Erasmus added a further idea to it—that even outside the Jewish world the Spirit of God had done great things, and had evoked words of wisdom and ideas full of the Spirit, pointing to Christ. In his time these words were of great importance. Particularly significant, I believe, is the basic statement to be found in the *Convivium religiosum*: 'Perhaps the Holy Spirit is poured forth more widely than we think. And in the communion of saints there are many who do not appear in our calendar.' Erasmus' concern with mastering Greek and Hebrew in order to go back to the original text of the Bible and the Fathers of the Church, spring from this conviction that he could find Christ himself in everything that was of positive value, and thus serve the unity of the Church. This is related to a second strand in his humanism, his: *Readiness for friendship and for correspondence.* Much could be said here about his noble and inspiring letters. Instead of a critical examination I should prefer to cite just one letter, as a record of a friendship. It is the letter to Ulrich von Hütten about Thomas More: 'If you ask me as it were to paint a picture of More . . . I should like to begin with what is least known about him. In form and stature of body he is slight, the colour of his skin is white, the face inclines more to brightness than to pallor . . . He is more inclined to joking than to seriousness and gravity . . . His health is more fortunate than sound . . . His speech is wonderfully clear and distinct. It has nothing overdone or halting about it . . . His main pleasure is to observe the form, peculiarities and feelings of the various forms of life. Thus there is hardly any species of bird he does not keep at home . . . He has taken great pains with his reading. When he was still almost a boy he gave public readings of Augustine's "City of God" . . . He directs his whole mind to the study of piety in vigils and prayer . . . All his family he rules with friendliness. He never sends anyone away as an enemy. His whole household seems destined for happiness . . . Amid the pressure of business he still thinks of old friends and often goes back to his beloved sciences . . . One can say that More is somehow the public protector of all the weak. He believes he has hit upon a large profit if he has raised someone oppressed, set free someone in bondage, or restored a man fallen from favour . . . And he is like this at the Court also. That is

why there are people who believe that Christians are not
found only in monasteries.'

That Erasmus should send such a letter about a Catholic
saint to a man whose position at that time was very dubious,
is particularly characteristic of his attitude of mind.
Everywhere he wanted to reconcile contradictions. And
this was the third distinguishing mark of his humanism:

The joining together of opposites. Of course More as
well as Erasmus *knew how to laugh.* Gaiety, mockery and
wit—all were a help in finding their mental balance. For
both of them this lightness was anything but levity. Fundamentally both were by nature brooding and ascetic. Their
cheerfulness was the infallible sign of self-mastery.
Thomas More displayed this cheerfulness unforgettably
when he spoke to his executioners at his execution. With
Erasmus it was the good humour with which he patiently
confronted his opponents and enemies—always ready for
discussion and encounter. Erasmus always wanted to join
everything together. This was the great opportunity of his
life, but also his tragedy.

I should like to draw attention again to something very
important: never before had Europe disposed of such an
élite of cultured men devoted to learning. The universi-
ties, the great publishers, the printers and their collabor-
ators brought together highly qualified scholars. The
great crisis that arose in Europe was at first only a crisis
of growth. It was a matter of integrating the fulness of
spirit that was breaking out in conflicting opinions and
outlooks into a greater community which offered room for
all to put forward their concerns and needs, and not least
to represent their vocation. In a greater Europe, in a
broader Church, there would have been a place for all of

them. But when the storm broke, Erasmus himself was afraid.

Hearts and minds were not yet ready to recognize the goodwill and freedom of a wit which, under cover of a fool's cap of mockery, sought to reveal a deep love for everything human. These men who sought a great reconciliation, to create peace among opponents, were victorious only in shipwreck and disaster. They all died overstrained and overloaded. Physical death usually followed an accusation—after denunciation, hatred and scorn had struck them all during their lifetime. But they were the seeds from which Europe lives.

It is remarkable how Erasmus stood aside from every camp in the great controversy; how he did not want to take sides; how he held to the centre. Reformers and Catholics sought his favour. Erasmus' relationship to both —and he refused them both—shows how indispensable he found the idea of the invisible Church, if he was to remain a good Christian. Today, after the Second Vatican Council, it is not so difficult for us to assess the figure of Erasmus. I am not surprised that it is now possible to write a history of ideas which, from the point of view of important conflicts and decisions associated with Erasmus' name, touches on almost everything that has happened since his time. But from these basic ideas I must draw out something at the root of his spirit.

The idea of peace. In one of his last *Colloquies* Erasmus attacked war in a sharp polemic, with a power of conviction and beauty of phrase otherwise found only in his major works. Even though one can recognize and reconstruct the actual historical and political situation from which these writings on peace arose, the Erasmus who speaks to us here stands outside history. Two pieces can be considered particularly in this context, the *Handbook of a Christian Prince* and the *Complaint of Peace*.

In the first he warns: 'About one thing only I should like to warn Princes bearing the Christian name, to give up pretexts and seriously and with their whole heart seek that there be an end to the fury of war, and that peace and concord be instituted among them, who are bound together in so many things. To that they should bend their minds, for that put forth their strength, for that give counsel, and toward that guide the efforts of all. Those who strive to appear great should also prove themselves to be great . . . We are all rushing upon our destruction. If we could make common cause according to common counsel, then each man's personal interest would flourish also. Now, however, even that for which alone we are fighting is lost.'

In the *Complaint of Peace* Erasmus spoke still more plainly, when he wrote of 'The Soldier's "Our Father" ', as follows: 'How can a soldier pray the Our Father at a service in the field? Shameless and loud-mouthed as you are, you dare to call on God as Father, while you put a knife to your brother's throat? Hallowed be thy name. How could God's name be dragged deeper into the mud than by mutual slaughter? Thy kingdom come. You pray thus, and at the same time want to set up your tyranny with streams of blood? Thy will be done, on earth as it is in heaven. God wills peace. Are you not seeking pretexts for war? You ask the Father of us all for daily bread. But do you not none the less scorch and burn down the crops of your brothers, because you would rather perish in misery than let them have any benefit from them? How do you pray, Forgive us our trespasses, as we forgive those who trespass against us, while you are setting out to murder your brother? In your prayer you want to keep away the danger of temptation. But do you not seek, at the risk of your own life, to lure your brother into a trap? Do you not demand to be delivered from the very evil you are preserving when you launch the most shameful attacks on your brother?'

Here I have to penetrate deeper into the spirit of Erasmus. He was no pacifist in the present-day sense of the word. He was much more—a promoter of what one might call a 'dialogue of enemies'. Erasmus had a deep understanding of the intellectual rôle of the mediator. I can describe his basic attitude in the following way: from the beginning there must be recognition of the indestructible values of the other side. The so-called 'enemy'—a person, a group, a church, a party—at first refuses a dialogue, but has the right for this to be respected by us. The enemy's resistance sets off a storm within us.

This inner storm provides an important insight for Erasmus. Dialogue between foes is basic, and has to be constantly reopened within one's own self. The lines of division run through ourselves, and the dialogue must first be an internal one. In this inward dialogue with the 'enemy within', if it is carried through and not broken off, an illumination and clarification is experienced that teaches detachment and moderation.

From this grows the cardinal virtue of the open, Christian humanist in the world—patience. Erasmus realized that patience is everything. Often long periods must pass before there can be a 'dialogue of enemies'.

People cannot be expected to acquire overnight the taste for an open society, for the diversity of partner and opponent.

Erasmus knew very well how endlessly difficult dialogue is, as he imagined it. But for him trust in the power of the spirit created an *optimism* that is the basic strength of open, 'Erasmian' humanism. Optimism is the virtue of the devout who expose themselves—inspired by an insuperable trust—to daily shipwreck, to the crushing of the newly begun dialogue, even to the destruction of their own lives.

I do not know whether I can define correctly Erasmus' attitude of peace in its full depth. Four points must serve as a guide to the deepening of the Erasmian element in our Christianity. This is not idealization but a hard, sometimes painful realism of the faith. To give oneself up to history in which, at first, the spirit of God has been crucified and laid low, so as then to be re-born and achieve resurrection. 'Unless the seed die, it brings forth no fruit'. Perhaps this reaches to the depths in which Erasmus' whole stance in life is concentrated, his:

Idea of a third force. Everywhere in Erasmus' work, above all in his letters, we find this attitude of being active between the front lines, and persevering in meditation. Erasmus always wanted to live near to frontiers, which in an emergency he could cross within a few hours. Basically the life he led was that of a fugitive. He could not and would not put down lasting roots anywhere, except perhaps in England which, because of its geographical situation, was naturally somewhat cut off, and inclined to stand between the parties. But even Erasmus' love for England ended in sorrow and silence.

In the elation of 1509, when Erasmus experienced the accession of Henry VIII, he could still hope that More's attitude would not be an isolated case but would become a type, be multiplied, dominate English life and introduce a period of peace in Europe. Sixteen years later, when Henry had again led England back into the turbulence of continental wars, broken with the Catholic Church, and brought More, who for three years had been his chancellor, to the scaffold, Eramsus could have printed only in Basle, very quietly, the eyewitness account of his friend's death, a report of which had been brought to the Continent by fugitives from England.

I do not want to go at length into Erasmus' rôle, doomed to failure, as mediator between Rome and the Reformers. But it should be briefly recorded how he was consulted by both Rome and the Reformers, and unfortunately could register no success with either. In January 1523 Hadrian VI sent an urgent letter to him, asking for advice on the question of how he should act in the approaching storm. Erasmus wrote to the Pope in great haste a letter ending as follows: 'Now your Holiness will ask me: what must now be changed? To advise on these matters there should be summoned from each district men who are irreproachable, worthy, mild, beloved and dispassionate, whose judgment . . .' Here the letter breaks off in mid-sentence. But we can see from this fragmentary sentence what kind of reform of the Church, and what sort of procedure on the part of Rome, Erasmus would have preferred.

Also in 1523 Erasmus wrote to a friend: 'I have written to the Pope giving my advice. Now I am drawing back from the conflict and passing on to quieter matters.

In writing the Paraphrases [explanations of the Bible] I believe I am doing my best work, and no one is hurt by it.'
Just as Erasmus failed with his proposals for mediation, so the Pope suffered shipwreck with his programme of reform. He died on 14 September 1523, without having reached his goal.

Erasmus' at first very valuable friendship with Luther (and with other Reformers) also ended very tragically. A letter of his in this connexion seems significant: 'I pray to Christ our Lord that he may quieten a little Luther's style and soul, so that he may be of help to evangelical piety . . . Among his opponents I see a number who love the world more than Christ. Certainly there are sins on both sides . . . I wish that Luther would draw back from this struggle for a time, so that he could work, without being carried away by passion, for the gospel. At present he is all hatred against me, which does him great harm . . . Not every truth is good to speak, above all not at every time. But the style or way in which one speaks is important.'

In this situation there was a mysterious tragedy: Erasmus was seen as an enemy by both sides, although he was perhaps the one man who could have brought the two sides together.

From this hopeless position Erasmus eventually fled to the only man who could say of himself that he was our 'way', to Christ. That was his ultimate and deepest wisdom, the philosophy of Christ. In his *Admonitions on the Study of Christian Philosophy* he said: 'First one must know what Christ taught, then one must live it. I do not believe that a Christian may think himself to be a Christian if he discusses ingeniously every scholastic problem, but if he holds to and follows Christ's teaching and life . . . When a man of devout mind philosophizes, more praying than disputing, more concerned with moral renewal than intellectual armament, he will find that everything is allotted to him that belongs to human happiness . . . The gospels show you a Lord who speaks and heals, dies and rises again, and eventually they make him so much present to you, that you would see him less if he were before your eyes.'

Alas, these men of the 'third force' did not succeed. They were crushed between two millstones. They were known, and respected; but only today, in a time of extreme conflict, has their greatness of spirit been properly recognized. Their basic attitude of mind we must all, myself included, help to prevail today. Otherwise they will be lost, Erasmus most of all, to Christendom and to all mankind.

Gregory and beauty

Gregory and beauty

To every man God speaks his own language. To me—very plainly—he speaks the language of beauty. In this chapter the only principle I follow in selecting my thoughts is that they have especially pleased me, and moved me inwardly. I think that the concept of truth merges in the end with that of beauty. To a great extent that is also true of my faith. In the last analysis what moves me isn't 'the *truth* of what is believed', but its *beauty*. In other words: a truth that is beautiful deserves to be true.

Hans Urs von Balthasar, the theologian, has written a major work on 'Glory'. There he puts the question of beauty right at the centre of theological reflexion. His is the first really comprehensive attempt to show that God's revelation happens in an 'overpowering of the spirit', by its self-evident nature, by the radiance—the beauty—of Being: that is, of Glory. The beauty of Christ becomes a condition of the totality of Christian life, thought and action. Gabriel Marcel has reminded us of the two meanings of the word 'grace' in French: on the one hand, supernatural grace; on the other, beauty.

I am sure of this: if and in so far as a person follows his 'feeling for beauty' and more firmly, and refuses to put up with anything ugly in himself (whether in his acts, or in his ideas or his most secret thoughts), if he always holds himself open to the beautiful, then he will become more sensitive to truth. I allow myself to be 'charmed' by ideas, to be drawn by the spell of their beauty, even if they are transitory and imperfect.

In each thought I try above all to discover whatever means a victory over the ugliness in the world. Of course not every 'victory' of thought is final. Even in our most beautiful thoughts, much is transitory. But it is part of the greatness of an everlasting spirit to be able and willing to love transitory beauty too.

But it is not always thoughts that speak truth to us. More often it is the truth-radiating figures of spiritual men and women. Perhaps Francis of Assisi's eyes proclaimed his inner truth; or his hands from which help flowed so generously to his fellow men. One can scarcely overestimate the power of simple and humble contemplation of the form of truth as beauty. The beautiful inwardly nourishes the spirit, makes it receptive to existence and ready for the appearance of ultimate truth.

We must also follow the line of thought that shows how being returns to its source, being that springs from and into God. God lives as self-communication. His substance is pure relation: as Father; and, as his own knowledge of himself become a person, his Son; and between the two, springing from them both and eternally flowing between them, the Holy Spirit. In this eternal procession of the Trinity is founded all God's external creation.

More precisely, it is God's self-knowledge made a Person, the Logos, in which every image of God, every created thing, is rooted. God has created finite being from nothing else, from no other image and law, than from the eternal image of God himself, from the Second

Person of the Trinity. In our creatureliness we are in the midst of the eternal life of the Trinity. This origin in God establishes in men a drive towards God. In men God himself draws creation into the sphere reserved for himself of purity, imperishability, value and joy. Accordingly there is no 'profane' sphere in our world, outside the realm of the holy, neither within ourselves nor in our environment. The 'atmosphere of being' in the world is pure.

If one tries to go more deeply into this original source of being and life, in an intellectual way, there arises a deep joy, a cheerfulness of spirit which I can best characterize as 'adoration'. Here too the meaning of 'God is love' (1 John 4:8) is apparent. God is he who streams forth from the intimacy of his absolute being, in the freest commitment, so that something outside himself shall exist. Gregory of Nyssa indicates this in his *Commentary on the Song of Songs*: 'It is as with the jugs from which anointing oil has been poured out, and the type of oil that has been poured is no longer recognizable in its essence. Nevertheless we form ideas about the oil that has been poured out from certain indications, from the odour that remains in the jug. This is what we learn here: what the oil of God is in its essence goes beyond all names and concepts. But the marvels we see in the universe form the material for the names we give to God, such as wise, or mighty, good, holy, blessed, eternal, Judge and Saviour, and others besides. All this, however, is only an insignificant fragment of the oil of God of which the whole creation bears the imprint.'

I should like to clarify these references by considering the example of a Father of the Church—Gregory of

D

Nyssa. He was a sympathetic, but truly strange, man. It is not known with certainty when and where he was born, nor when and where he died. We know that at first he wanted to be a priest, but then decided on marriage and became a rhetorician. His 'strong' brother, St Basil the Great, had almost to force him to become a bishop, in order to assist him. By inner disposition Gregory was a poet, but he had to 'practise' theology. By nature he was an introvert but he had to enter Church politics. He was persecuted and driven out of his diocese, but at the second Council of Nicaea he was hailed as the 'father of the Fathers'. Such were the tensions amid which lived one of the most important but also most individual thinkers of the age of the Fathers. I want here first to give a short sketch of what we know of his life. It is very little, but at least supplies an outer framework within which he can be understood.

Gregory, son of Basil the Elder and Emmelia, was probably born in Caesarea about the year 335. It was a family firm in its faith, one might almost say a 'holy family'. His father and mother, Basil and his wife Emmelia, are honoured as saints. Three sons became bishops, all three are saints: Basil the Great, Gregory of Nyssa and Peter of Sebastopol. A daughter, Macrina, was also reckoned a saint. Basil the Great was the eldest son, and watched over the upbringing of his younger brothers and sisters. Gregory was at first attracted to the priesthood and achieved the office of 'lector' (reader). But at that time nothing came of it. He married one Theosebia and became a professor of Literature, a 'rhetor'.

In face of the vigorous reproaches of his friends, above all a good friend of the family, Gregory of

Nazianzen, he returned to the solitude of the monastic life. It was only under pressure that he accepted the bishopric forced on him by his brother Basil. In 371 he was consecrated Bishop of Nyssa in Cappadocia by his brother. He had probably kept his wife with him during all this time. At least, a reference in the documents points to this. In the difficulties of practical life in the Church Gregory had in part failed. He was even condemned and deposed by a Synod. After the death of the Emperor Valens, in the year 378, he returned to Nyssa as bishop. In his exile he seems to have turned to the thoughts of his brother Basil.

At almost the same time that he won back his diocese, an event occurred that determined his whole destiny. His brother Basil died on 1 January 379. Gregory became his heir in all respects: in theology, in monastic questions, and also in matters of ecclesiastical politics. It seems that this event made him fully conscious of his responsibility. Basil was a great, I might even say 'too great', personality. This had apparently given Gregory a marked inferiority complex. Certainly Basil was very fond of him, had even loved him. But he never properly recognized his value. Now that Gregory had to assert himself on his own, his personality developed and he reached the true depths of his thought.

The Synod of Antioch entrusted him (in 379) with the visitation of the diocese of Pontus, and at this time he was appointed Metropolitan of Sebastopol, where he had to spend some months in what he himself described as 'Babylonian captivity'. At the Council of Constantinople he was revered for his orthodoxy. But soon after his visit to the Council he died. Exactly where and when, as has already been mentioned, is not known. In his final period his activity at the Emperor's Court was highly valued. He delivered the funeral oration on the death of the Empress Flaccilla and her daughter Pulcheria, in 386.

But Gregory's gifts were more evident in his meditative writings. Superior as a philosopher and theologian to the other 'Cappadocians', Basil the Great and Gregory of Nazianzen, his great merits lay above all in the philosophical analysis of the teachings of faith. But Gregory was very closely connected with Origen in his teaching, and took over from him and defended doctrines for which Origen was condemned as a heretic, for example, the 'non-perpetuity of hell'. Here I shall confine myself to a single work of Gregory of Nyssa, which is not, it is true, among the most important, but which best condenses his spiritual teaching—the commentary on the Song of Songs. I should like to select four salient points from these fifteen homilies: the characterizing of all creation as image; the everlasting progress of man; the idea of the fulfilment of the universe; and the darkness of God.

One of Gregory's basic perceptions was that God is infinitely great; yet men not only recognize him, but are aware of him as the Lord who is close at hand.

This is possible because all creation is an image. I have already quoted the text with which Gregory interprets the beginning of the Song of Songs ('Your name is anointing oil poured out', Song of Solomon, 1 : 3). He at once seizes on this idea, with all its inner tensions—that God is far from us ('poured out') and yet the whole world 'tastes' of him.

The idea of eternal progress without doubt forms the core of his teaching: 'The vision of God consists in the

soul never tiring in its longing to lift up its eyes to God'.
And 'The whole of creation cannot go outside itself, in a
comprehensive act of knowledge. It remains always within
itself. Whatever it looks at it sees itself. It is incapable
of seeing anything other than its self . . . In the world of
light it cannot transcend itself limitlessly.' It is not surprising that over Gregory's whole theology there floats
something like a breath of mourning.

Gregory actually spoke of the vision of God in his
exposition of the 'blessedness of those that mourn'. Here,
in the commentary on the Song of Songs, God is called
the 'hopeless beauty', 'See what seeing means: not-
seeing!' I am really tempted to say that Gregory's thinking
was dominated by a titanic, all-enveloping spirit, a spirit
that knew peace only in disquiet, happiness only in desperation. With him even the vision of God is built upon
the being of the creature. But can the ultimate meaning
of the creature be found only in its movement towards
God? I must not try to classify Gregory of Nyssa too
hastily. Is that the whole of Gregory's teaching about
God? By no means!

We are God's thoughts. This means a kind of 'blood
relationship' with God himself. Human longing for God
is aroused by the thought of an eternal likeness to him.
The gulf seems to be bridged in a marvellous way. Without the previous statement becoming untrue (i.e., that the
creature's vision is limited ultimately to self-vision),
God is mysteriously transferred into the inner being of
the creature. The soul formed by grace sees, as it looks
within itself, as in a mirror, its origin, God himself. The
more it is purified by God, the more it can be gripped by
the divine purity.

This solution is reminiscent of the philosophy of Leibniz: the soul, with no external windows, mirrors within itself the eternal light. God is seen 'in the transparency of the heart'. The soul is a mirror of God, and the purer it becomes, the greater and purer is our vision of God himself.

Now we cannot fail to perceive what Gregory of Nyssa's whole theology is leading to—God's incarnation as man. Christ took on our human nature. Through him all men stand in immediate, ontological communion with God. Thus the closed 'monads' are broken open. They are opened out from within by grace. However, the Incarnation will only be completed when all humanity, in all its branches, is made transparent to grace, when mankind has become the body of Christ: 'When the Good has poured itself out in everything, then the whole body will be subject to the life-giving power . . . then Christ will cease to build up himself . . . Then all creation will be but a single body.'

It can be seen why Gregory came out in favour of the non-finality of hell, with Origen and some later Greek fathers.

Throughout the whole of Gregory's commentary on the Song of Songs, there is an urge to go further, to break out. The hope of another world inspires his whole work and activity: 'A blessedness is promised us, that exceeds our yearning; a gift that exceeds our hope; a grace that exceeds our nature.' What we have now is the sign given in the Song of Songs—'your name is oil poured out'.

I must be quite honest here. Have we much more than this? Don't we sense a little of the divine in our life without really knowing who or what it is that we are meeting?

I have left aside here everything in the *Commentary on the Song of Songs* that is rhetorical repetition and ornament, and traced out only the essential line of thought.

Only thus is it possible to disclose what is most beautiful, and also largely unknown, in the work of Gregory, the quiet, modest monk and bishop, who only became a monk and a bishop reluctantly, and nonetheless, or rather therefore, was called the 'father of the Fathers'. I am convinced that we must make his insights our own. In their depth they are true and important for our life.

I should like to develop further Gregory's basic thinking, and to explain his idea of:

Man's constant progress. This is how a man can understand the saying, 'Arise . . . and come away; for lo, the winter is past, the rain is over and gone. The flowers appear on the earth . . .' Gregory interprets this passage from the Song of Songs: Someone speaks to us; but it is simply the *voice* of the one desired that is revealed, to the hearing only, not in full perception: 'It is not the form, not the countenance, that reveals the being of him who is sought, but the voice. It is more a surmise than a certainty . . . He is coming, but not stopping, not staying so that the searching eye can recognize him, but escaping its glance . . . What is momentarily grasped is always something else . . . "Arise . . . and come away!" Nature had been frozen by the service of idols . . . But when the sun rose and brought spring, it released nature from its bonds and warmed the whole landscape with its rising radiance . . . And from then on it has been thus: it is impossible for anyone who truly rises to cease to rise, or for him who runs to the Lord to cease running. For the course he runs is never finished. There is always more rising, and never a rest from running. And as often as God repeats his cry, "Arise and come", he gives the power to arise.'

This idea balances that which preceded it, although it is a continuation of it. God is grasped in a ceaseless ascent of the soul, in the never-faltering yearning of existence. Gregory says: 'It seems to me that there is much that man understands of God, but infinitely more that lies beyond what is understood . . . Man does indeed see God, but always only as much as he can perceive, according to his strength. The boundlessness and incomprehensibility of the Godhead lies beyond all conception . . . When we look up God is always the same height above us . . . I believe the man running towards God grows ever further and higher beyond himself . . . What is newly grasped is eternally greater than what has already been understood, and yet it never encloses what is sought for, but the boundaries of what has been discovered become the starting point of further search. The climber never stands still, he receives beginning upon beginning.'

Gregory goes on: 'Perhaps the soul has nothing more with which to raise itself higher. For it has moulded itself feature by feature according to God—source to source, life to life. Living is God's word, living too the soul that receives the word . . . But the soul is in a way stricken by the hopelessness of its earthly thirsting. Its veil of mourning, however, is ripped away when it learns that it is precisely the eternal progress in the search, and the never-resting ascent that are the true quenching of longing, when every longing fulfilled to the brim produces a fresh yearning for God. Once it has thus thrown aside the mantle of hopelessness and looked down on the hopeless-indescribable beauty of God, it awakens to the ever greater glory it has found, and stretches forth in powerful thirst.'

And then another profession of faith: 'What has not yet been found is always more beautiful than what has already been grasped.'

Finally there is this central passage: 'There is only one way for the spirit to recognize the overflowing power of God—never to rest on what has been grasped, but to seek increasingly for the more that still lies out of reach . . . God is the soul's way out and way in. Way out from that we are, and way in to the possessions that lie before us . . . The going in will never end, and therefore the going out, too, will never cease. By continual going in, our going out will rise constantly above what is already known.'

According to Gregory, therefore, the endless movement of the spirit is an endless movement of new beginning from God to God. This movement goes eternally upwards and onwards, an endless ascent. The mounting flight of the spirit forms the basic movement of our lives, which of its nature continues into all eternity: 'The soul will never attain completion because it will never reach its limit . . . Since God of his nature is boundless, community of nature with him must be boundless and always capable of receiving more.'

God and the soul are moulded to each other like the *eternally flowing stream* and the *eternally thirsting drinker*. From this 'rhythm of being', this 'inter-penetration of things', rings out the 'true and original music of divine wisdom'. Fuller participation and greater openness here coincide. Openness in longing—according to Gregory this is the deepest essence of man.

Now however I must take up with him the question of the *perfection of the universe*. In such a world can anyone

really be damned? Can there be an everlasting hell?
Gregory answers (for himself alone, I must emphasize)
with a decisive No: 'One is the King, Lord of all creation.
He rules over the darkness also. Princes and powers stand
under the King of Kings and Lord of Lords . . . the
Princes and powers will only be swept away when evil
disappears into nothingness.'

He continues: 'Our existence began from perfection.
When it then . . . fell away it did not at once regain perfection. It advanced only gradually upwards . . . God
raises up each man according to his various efforts . . .
Such seems to us to be the meaning of Scripture, where
it is written, God will be all in all. He will fuse all together in the unity of faith, in Christ Jesus, our Lord.'

At this point Gregory puts forward a fine interpretation of the parable of the Good Samaritan: 'This is the
one we seek, because he was my brother and also a neighbour to the man who fell among thieves and whose
wounds he healed with oil and wine and bandages . . . As
the first born of mankind he took to himself all human
nature, including every nation. He came bodily to where
the man had fallen, healed his wounds, lifted him
onto his own beast, put him up in his own house, which
is friendly to men and where all the weary and heavily
laden are received. Whoever takes him in takes in also the
one who comes with him . . . When a man takes him into
his own homestead, he turns himself into a house for the
infinite.'

Christ appears here in the image of the Good Samaritan,
who takes humanity into his own dwelling place. Thus
the 'incomprehensible' can happen, that men, and according to Gregory of Nyssa all men, themselves become

dwelling places of the infinite, habitations of God.

Then comes another central text : 'The eye of man never sees God in his full greatness, but only as far as the eye can comprehend him . . . Thus the wanderer never pauses in his climb . . . The springs of goodness draw him who thirsts ever onward. Neither the thirst nor the course of the longing nor the pleasure of drinking will have an end, but there is an eternal demand to thirst and drink and run towards God . . . Thus the climber is never without the impulse drawing him on to greater things.'

If I consider all these references from Gregory of Nyssa then I see the image of a God who can also be king over evil because he seeks out this evil where it is wounded and can give it too an everlasting, saving destiny. Although to me personally such a picture of God is most sympathetic, I should be careful not to depict God in this way to my fellow men and friends. I wonder whether such an outlook does not endanger the radical freedom of the creature. Perhaps there is still a possibility of saying, God damns no one, only the creature can allot himself damnation. The possibility of hell is accordingly affirmed. It remains to be established whether any man has ever actually made this possibility a reality. This approach would, in my view, be in accordance with the Church's teaching, but without conjuring up the picture of a God who damns.

Finally I must describe a fourth basic idea of Gregory of Nyssa :

The mystery of darkness. In any case it is enough for me to say, we are able to know that God loves us in a way that we could not, from our hearts. 'For God is greater than our hearts' (1 John 3 : 20). We cannot think largely enough, nor with enough goodness, nor forgivingly

enough. How in the end God joins everything together
is not our affair. It is enough for us to know that his
goodness is greater than we could imagine for ourselves.
I believe that Gregory of Nyssa means to indicate this idea,
when he speaks of God as the 'one who is found yet
cannot be found': 'The human spirit is in a certain sense
created ever anew. It changes into something higher
through growth in goodness. No further shore is visible
for it, it is bounded by no frontier . . . What could give
greater happiness than the vision of God? Each enters into
the other. God enters the soul and the soul goes forth into
God. It says, my beloved is in me and I am in him. What
can there be beyond that—oneself to be in the desired one,
and to hold the desired one within oneself? And yet, the
soul begins again to complain, as if it had been robbed of
the good . . . Here we must consider—God's glory is not
limited by any boundary. And therefore there is no degree
of knowledge at which forward movement can stop . . .
The perfection of knowledge again becomes a starting
point for a higher longing . . . In this the soul discovers
that it is as far from reaching perfection as one who has
not even begun . . . And so it arises anew, and traverses
nature in its thoughts, where there are principalities and
powers . . . lest perhaps the beloved might be found
among these. It searches through all the orders of angels,
and when it does not find him among the goods discovered,
says to itself, can he really be found, my beloved? It asks
everyone, have you perhaps seen him whom I love? But
people are silent in reply, and their silence means that they
too cannot grasp what the soul is seeking. The soul then
leaves what it has found . . . and recognizes the one it is
seeking as he who is known by not being known . . . It

says to itself, scarcely had I abandoned what I had, and renounced every concept, when I found my beloved in faith. I shall not let him go, him I found in faith and now still hold.'

Gregory conceived the Christian life as 'return', as 'creation anew' of an original state, as a 'reversal' of time to the state of original justice. But his system is by no means exhausted by these definitions. On the contrary, a man must always advance towards a more beautiful, more perfect good. Here one has to distinguish (approximately) six elements:

First: *expectation.* There have been few people who looked less into the past than Gregory of Nyssa. He constantly quotes St Paul: 'Brethren, I do not consider that I have made it my own; but one thing I do, forgetting what lies behind and straining forward to what lies ahead, I press on toward the goal for the prize of the upward call of God in Christ Jesus.' (Phil. 3 : 13–14.)

One must take note here of the reference to the parousia: to expectation and to hope. The soul waits for the revelation of God in his greatness. All creation is intent upon this revelation. Hope is like the stick with which the blind man feels his way ahead. The 'land of dreams' is not 'below' but above, where no feeling reaches, where 'we ourselves shine with the eternal light, Jesus Christ'. The nostalgia for a 'lost Paradise' is replaced, for Gregory of Nyssa, by the longing for the 'kingdom to come'.

Secondly: *transcending time.* Gregory reflected often on the perishability of human life. Life is time spent 'beneath a tent', brief, transitory. The monastic life seemed to him a hastening of the 'end of time', in which a man could bring forth more fruit at death. A curious line of thought, which seems even more profound if you consider the argument for it. You do not interpose any link between yourself and the coming of Christ. You pass over, transcending time, immediately into God. You are already at your goal. Gregory gave an example of this way of life, when he praised the young monks: 'I have found many among them who, despite their youth, have become mature and have already overtaken their youth in their life.' This example seems to be intended to show that the true Christian life not only overtakes youth but reaches out into eternity.

Thirdly: *the last days*. The Christian life is already an anticipation of the 'last things'. One already gathers, 'in this life, the fruits of Resurrection'. Indeed one already acquires the 'heavenly life'. 'To measure oneself to the divine life is a science'. 'Through the sacrifice of one's own life one begins today already to lead the life of the angels.' This is a life that represents 'the summit of all hope and the goal of all longing' and likewise the 'essence of all God's promises'. Thus it becomes clear that the Christian life is a fulfilment of Christ's resurrection.

Fourthly: *eternity*. People often reproach Gregory with elevating mystic contemplation in his life, and making it so important that the 'vision of God in eternity' receives only a minor, supplementary significance. It is indeed true that according to Gregory there is an inner connexion between our vision of God in prayer and our eternal blessedness. But for Gregory the decisive event in our eternity is that Christ will become 'all in all'. It is the 'coming of God' that changes everything and yet preserves everything that is worth preserving. 'All that the prophets longed for, that the kings and virgins imagined, and everything, too, that we have already hoped for, will be realized; man will see God.'

Fifthly: But how, according to Gregory, is this 'vision of God' possible at all? God is purity, indestructibility, light and beauty. All this makes him unapproachable by us. Gregory proclaims with great insistence that 'God cannot be grasped', that we can 'express him neither with words nor with concepts', that he 'totally exceeds our knowledge'. You can, it is true, be aware of God when you contemplate his deeds in history, although in his essence he exceeds all contemplation. Hence the soul itself can become beautiful as it approaches the eternal beauty: 'It grows full of light, as it participates in the true light . . . When we climb up out of our darkness, we ourselves become light, as we approach the true light.'

Now comes the formulation in which Gregory sums up his whole theology: 'We know the unlike through the like.' God is 'mirrored' in created things. The soul itself is created 'in his image'. So it must also be possible to perceive God within the soul. Eternal beauty shows itself just as grandly within a man as in the heights of heaven. Man is related to God. 'The soul's likeness to God is . . . the kingdom of God within you.' All injunctions 'to find oneself' and to 'return to oneself' can now be seen no longer as self-reflexion but as searching for God. This search for God is bound to have its effects. The soul that has made itself beautiful, pure and full of light can grasp God, because it has become like him. This 'taking hold of God', of 'like by like', is the real basis of the spirituality of Gregory of Nyssa.

Sixthly: *speaking of God*. I wonder what a man can say about God? Gregory says plainly, 'Every man is a liar . . . not indeed out of hatred or wickedness, but because of the weakness of his powers of expression.' But Paul 'saw things of which no man can speak'. If we take this admission of incapability seriously, then there remains for us only silence. Hence Gregory preserves the inexpressibility of God, and yet stresses the possibility of experiencing God. He takes up into his theology the old theme 'know yourself' and transfers it to the knowledge and preaching of God.

When I consider all this, then I find myself repeating the great 'Hymn to God' that says more about the inexpressibility of God than many learned essays. This hymn has been ascribed to Gregory of Nazianzen, to Gregory of Nyssa, and to Proclus. I do not think this matters much since all three moved in the same spheres of thought: 'O you beyond all things! Is this not all that can be said of you? What hymn would speak in language proper to you? No word expresses you. Of what should the mind take hold? You transcend all understanding! You alone are inexpressible, for everything that can be said comes from you. You alone are unfathomable, for everything that can be thought comes from you. All beings, whether thinking or unthinking, do you honour. The yearning of the universe, the sighs of the universe, rise up to you. All that is prays to you, and every being thought of in your world lets rise to you a hymn of silence. All that endures, endures through you. In you rests the movement of the universe. You are the goal of all beings. You are each being. And yet you are no single one of them. Nor are you their totality. You are not a single existing thing.

And you are not the totality of things. All names belong to you. But what shall I call you, you whom one cannot name? What heavenly mind will ever be able to penetrate the mist that veils heaven itself? Have pity! O you, beyond everything! Is not this everything that one can say of you?'

The notion of God, constantly threatened and almost extinguished, grows in and with us, ever anew. It seems as if everything will destroy it. But the very thing that seems to destroy it, gives it fresh nourishment. Man will never be finished with his confrontation with God. The mysterious and unequal struggle about God and with God will last for a long time, perhaps until the end of time, through the whole long night of our history: 'O Lord my God, lighten my eyes, lest I sleep the sleep of death'. (Psalms 13:3.)

I have to thank Gregory for showing me the unfathomable beauty of God, and the beauty of human thought, while retaining the courage to present it as mystery.

Aquinas and harmony

Aquinas and harmony

Patient composure and dedication to thinking in beauty, in so far as I have experienced and tried to practise them, have filled me with a tranquil joy. In them I have experienced the 'sanctity' of the world, the security of my own existence in the goodness of God, shining through all reality. I experienced this joy repeatedly as a special, direct approach of God to men. It transported me temporarily to a height from which I could see into the joy and sorrow of existence not only in its threatening reality but in its transitoriness.

I have experienced this joy not as a 'message' or a 'profession'. I wanted not so much to tell my joy to others, as simply to let it resound, and thus help lighten burdens and liberate. My joy was seldom cheerful and carefree. It is difficult to say in what it consisted. Perhaps in this: quiet, inner joy, in which grave matters seemed to float easily and, at the same time, slighter things to weigh more heavily. The sun shone, but it did not blaze, consume and burn. The sky arched over the earth but did not burden it, did not press upon it. In my joy something happened that was rather like what Karl Barth says about Mozart: 'A glorious disturbance of the accustomed balance of the world, in the force of which the light intensifies and the shadows, without completely disappearing, fade; gaiety overtakes sorrow, without extinguishing it; the Yes comes to sound stronger than the still present No. In it life seems a game already won, at a certain height or depth, and perfection a plea already fulfilled in advance, mercy sought as if it were long since found.'

I write these lines in the conviction that one day a time will come when what is now loud will be silent. All that is visible, palpable and audible, all that is not supported by a still centre, will one day be pushed aside into a margin of feebleness or non-existence. What is as yet silent, or unprepared for the struggle, will emerge as strong. What today is hidden will become plain as the decisive element. There must come a condition of the world—flowing out from the world itself and yet at the same time 'descending' as an undeserved gift from heaven—in which intention will be more important than deed. Essential character will weigh more heavily than success.

Here I have kept silent on some things for which the time has not yet come, or for which I'm not yet ready. Perhaps I may invoke here the great passage in Dante's *Divine Comedy*, where the poet meets the great men of antiquity in limbo, is accepted into their circle and honoured with confidential conversations 'of which it is good to be silent'.

A particular characteristic of this inner joy in the sphere of thought is 'harmony'. It is glorious and at the same time full of grace. You suddenly feel that everything 'fits'. Thoughts fit together quietly and calmly. All at once you notice the still glow of truth. At the same time you feel instinctively that it simply 'must be so' and that you can live according to this truth. It is the grace-filled correspondence of thought and life, of the course of ideas with a particular standpoint in life.

In this way a person becomes a 'lived truth'. And a truth which not only exists in itself but benefits others, which sets free goodness and radiates it into the world. This feeling always arises in me when I am occupied with the works of Thomas Aquinas and consider the person who stands behind them. I want to describe, in terms of his work and life, what I have just been talking about.

Of course it is presumptuous to give a short account of the life and work of Thomas Aquinas. His life dispensed with the brightness of colour of other thinkers and saints. His biographers were almost confined to a knowledge of his external career. Only rarely did Thomas supply them with an insight into his inner life. He shrank almost fearfully from entrusting his inner experiences to others. What his friends and pupils have to report about him seems somewhat cliché-ridden. While it is largely possible to point out the progress and development of his work, it is almost impossible to trace the unfolding of his character. His first biographers were only concerned to fit Aquinas' life into a pre-existing scheme. They were also very efficient at excluding anything that helps one to draw conclusions about his real spiritual struggles and the development of his personality. It's like standing before a Russian icon, its features fixed and in a hieratic posture. And yet to me these oldest accounts are particularly valuable because, through the clichés, I am able to sense the lonely greatness of that great thinker.

The astonishing richness of his work, which for decades has exercised a decisive influence on me, tempt me to enquire into his life, although it is almost hopeless to attempt a really accurate biography of him as a saint.

So I should like, because I am attracted precisely by the seemingly impossible, to approach the personality of Aquinas indirectly. First I propose to depict the outer framework of his life. Then, in a second part, to expound what seems to me the core of his teaching. Finally I want to unfold from this core the structure of his personality. I know that my portrayal will not achieve the brilliance of other accounts. But I hope to be able to work out something that is indispensable in the intellectual field: the peace and security of a hidden but unusual life. The harmony of life and work in Thomas Aquinas was so great that I could not better illustrate it from any other life.

A quiet life. Thomas Aquinas was not the son of a count, nor was his family, as has often been asserted, related to royalty on either the father's or the mother's side. He sprang from the lesser nobility. His father, Landulf of Aquino, Lord of Roccasecca, was appointed Justice of the 'Terra di Lavoro' by the Emperor Frederick II. In about 1225 Landulf had a child by his second marriage—his wife was of Norman stock—who received the baptismal name of Thomas. Landulf's family seem to have been fertile. From two marriages Landulf apparently had twelve children.

On both his father's and his mother's side, Thomas therefore belonged to the new peoples who had made their way into the Roman Empire and become heirs to its ancient culture. His father and relations served with the Emperor Frederick II and Thomas thus came early into contact with the world of the Hohenstaufen emperor.

Thomas' childhood was overshadowed by the struggle

between the two universal powers, the papacy and the Empire. Around 1230 Landulf brought his youngest son, Thomas, into the neighbouring abbey, Monte Cassino. It had already long since become clear to Landulf that he could do nothing better with his seventh son Thomas than to make him an abbot or 'something similar'. From childhood onwards Thomas had a mysterious aversion from everything suitable for the nobility: falconry, jousting and similar occupations. He was a large, clumsy and quiet boy, unusually silent, who hardly ever opened his mouth.

After barely ten years, however, he had to leave the quiet of the cloister. An open rift had once more broken out between the Emperor and Pope Gregory IX. In these circumstances the Abbot himself, Stephen of Corviano, advised the young Thomas to leave Monte Cassino and begin in Naples the study of the liberal arts.

We know little of his life at the University of Naples. The Emperor Frederick was trying to train his officials in his own territory. To remove them from foreign influence he established a university for them at Naples. Something happened there that was very important for the future life of Thomas Aquinas. In Naples, by contrast with Paris, it was possible to study the works of Aristotle without any Church prohibition. This study left a decisive imprint on Aquinas' whole thought and intellectual formation.

Still more decisive was the influence of the new mendicant Order of Dominicans, which he also came to know in Naples. So far as we can be clear about these rather confused events, it looks as if one day the young Thomas came to his father's castle and there quietly declared that he had become a mendicant friar in the new Order which the Spaniard Dominic had founded. Chesterton comments in his *St Thomas Aquinas* that it was '. . . much as the eldest son of the squire might go home and airily inform the family that he had married a gypsy; or the heir of a Tory Duke state that he was walking to-morrow with the Hunger Marchers organized by alleged Communists.'

There was no opposition to his entering monastic life, but his family had dreamed of seeing him one day Abbot of Monte Cassino. His brothers seized him on his way to Orvieto and abducted him to the fortress of Montesangiovanni Campano. After two years he was released. The family let Thomas have his way. He returned to Naples and was sent by his superiors in the Order to study abroad.

The older biographers do not make it clear whether Thomas was sent immediately to Cologne or whether he went first to Paris. I do not want to discuss here the various hypotheses, which can in no way be proved. Irrespective, however, of whether one assumes Thomas spent seven years of study in Cologne or only four, it is certain that it was Albert the Great, in Cologne, who was the first to understand the special quality of his pupil, protected him from the others and emphatically promoted his talent. We know for certain, at any rate, that Thomas left Italy in 1245.

Albert the Great was much too good a teacher not to know that the so-called 'dumb' pupils do not always need to stay that way. He heard with amusement how Thomas' fellow students used to call him the 'dumb ox'. All that seemed to him very natural. Aquinas was still known only as a particularly and persistently silent pupil among many far more brilliant and loquacious fellow students.

Albert the Great broke through this silence with the famous exclamation: 'You call him the dumb ox. But I tell you, the bellowing of this dumb ox will grow so loud that the whole world will hear it.' Thomas received from Albert the Great lasting support in his study of Aristotle.

In 1252 Thomas came to Paris as a graduate. He began his first lectures with an extended interpretation of Holy Scripture. The following year he had to give a new course on the 'sentences' of Peter the Lombard. Already in 1256 he was promoted to the position of 'Master' ('*Magister*') at the university college of Saint-Jacques.

Aquinas' teaching activity in Paris was at once over-shadowed by serious disputes. At the beginning there was the dispute over the right of members of the Order to teach at the university. The university hesitated to accept Thomas into its teaching body, and to recognize him as a Master, and even forbade attendance at his inaugural lecture.

Until the end of his stay in Paris he was engaged in drawing up one of his main future works, the *Summa contra Gentiles*, up to chapter 45 of the third book: that is, the first half.

Aquinas was to complete this work in Italy. After three years' work as a Master in Paris, he returned around the summer of 1259 first to Orvieto in Italy. In the autumn of 1265 he became Director of Studies at the Dominican house of Sta. Sabina in Rome. During his stay in Italy he began the composition of his *Summa Theologica*, which is regarded as his most important work, though Thomas actually wrote it as a textbook for students.

In the autumn of 1268 he was once again in Paris (his second period there), where he took the chair for foreign students at the Collège Saint-Jacques. There he worked further on his *Summa Theologica*, which however he was not able to finish. His four-year stay in Paris was again overshadowed by quarrels, this time on account of his Aristotelianism. Secular priests and Franciscans most of all were very much disturbed at the growing regard for Aristotle. After Easter 1272, when the University of Paris was on strike, the General of the Order recalled Thomas to Italy to organize a 'Studium generale' of theology.

Thomas chose Naples for this, or was perhaps called upon to do so by Charles I of Anjou, who wanted to reorganize the University of Naples. He was summoned to the Council of Lyons by Gregory X. He left Naples in February 1274, but died of a sudden illness on the way to Lyons, on 7 March 1274, in the Cistercian Abbey of Fossanuova. Biographers and witnesses agree in depicting his holy death and his readiness to submit himself and all his teaching to the Church. His life lasted just on fifty years.

After this necessarily dry and sketchy outline of the life I should like now to trace briefly the distinctive core of Aquinas' teaching.

The place of man in the doctrine of Thomas Aquinas. I want here to restrict myself to a single aspect of Aquinas' teaching, the place of the human person in his intellectual system. No doubt this is only a part of the system, but it is perhaps the most significant, and certainly the most decisive.

The objective order. For Aquinas, man is located in an objective order. His knowledge is not certain, but has to mirror the 'things of the world'. 'The order of truth corresponds to that of being' (*Summa contra Gentiles*, 1 : 1). His will moves in a world of objective norms. His inner impulses direct him to objective reality: 'In all capacities that relate to his own action, the action of the capacity in question must first be directed to an object' (*S.c.G.*, III : 26). The order of the world is projected within the person as a microcosm. The person therefore directs himself to an objective order of things even when he relates not to the world but only to himself.

In addition, if he recognizes the objective world and acts accordingly, then he directs his life to the greatest and highest reality, to God. So much is this objective orientation a part of him as a person that he recognizes even his own subjectivity in the light of objective reality (*S.c.G.*, III : 26). He is able to integrate the objective reality into his subjectivity, indeed is called upon to do so, so that his ego may be a 'form of the forms' of the world (*S.c.G.*, II : 47). Even his eternal happiness consists in 'possession' of the highest objective reality, in the vision of God. I can discover this predominance of the object in Thomas' system without great difficulty. But I have to be very careful in doing so. This simple formula does not seem adequate to the basic purpose of Thomas Aquinas.

The subjective order. If I am to do justice to the subtle concept of Thomas I must add, dialectically, to the formula I have just described. Human knowledge is a participation in the 'uncreated light, in which are contained the eternal bases of knowledge' (*S.Th.*, i, q. 84, a. 5, corp.). This light illuminates created things through the 'active intelligence'. In men even sensory perceptions take place in the light of God. Nor should I forget that the 'first principles' that regulate our whole intellectual activity are a participation in God's knowledge (cf. *De Ver.*, q. 8, a. 15, corp.), and that Thomas even speaks of them as 'inborn principles' (cf. *De Ver.* q. 11, a. 1, ad. 18 and *De Ver.* q. 11, a. 3, corp.). Thus man's similarity to God exceeds that of the world (*De Pot.*, q. 9, a. 8, corp.). I could pursue these reflexions further—for example into the question of the relationship between nature and the supernatural, where I could establish that for Thomas the supernatural plays a very decisive rôle in relation to nature—but what I have mentioned is enough to show how greatly Thomas emphasizes human subjectivity. In these two considerations I perceive a subtly woven doctrine concerning the human person.

It is true that objective reality stands above human subjectivity. At the same time, however, this objective reality itself is to be understood as a projective function of human subjectivity. The doctrinal stand of Aquinas is balanced between these two polar opposites and one cannot overload one side without inwardly destroying the whole system. From this complex attitude Thomas developed an approach to existence that has scarcely been realized until now, which I call the:

Attitude of balance. It is not by chance that Aquinas, in a time of upheaval very similar to our own, asked God that he might be 'cheerful without frivolity, and mature without self-importance' (*Oratio ad vitam sapienter instituendam. Opuscula theol.,* Turin-Rome, 1954, vol. 2, p. 285). Therefore opponents and opposing views were highly welcome to him. 'If anyone wants to write against this that will be very welcome to me. In no other way is truth better revealed and error better refuted than in resistance to contradiction' (*De perfectione vitae spiritualis*, end).

And so, according to Thomas Aquinas, both parties should always be heard: 'Just as in a court no one can deliver a judgment if he has not heard the cases for both parties, so the man who has to learn philosophy will necessarily judge better if he listens to all the reasons brought forward by doubting opponents' (in *Met.*, II : 1). Total openness was the condition for every discovery of truth. 'If anyone who claims for himself the name of "knowledge" wants to say something against what we have written here, he should not do it in a corner and before young boys who as yet have no judgment in such difficult matters, but should himself write against what has been written, if he dares' (*De unitate intellectus*, end). Truth should always be spoken, even in the face of the great and powerful: 'Truth does not change according to the high degree of him to whom it is spoken. He who speaks the truth cannot be defeated, no matter with whom he disputes' (in *Hiob.*, 13 : 2).

With a fine instinct he trusted to the progress of the mind: 'Knowledge grows. At first little is discovered. Thereafter this little will advance in great measure through the work of various people, since each adds what was lacking in the researches of his predecessors' (in *Eth.*, 1 : 1) or: 'The progress of knowledge takes place in two ways. In one way from the teacher's side, as he advances in knowledge in the course of time. And this is the basis of growth in knowledge that is based on human reason. And then, from the side of the pupil: The Master, who has command over his whole subject, does not deliver it all at once, at the beginning, to his pupils, because they could not grasp it, but only gradually, allowing for their capacity to understand. And in this way men have made progress in knowledge of the faith in the course of time' (*S.Th.*, II–II q. 1, a. 7, ad. 2).

Such insights were not agreeable in those days either. We know that Aquinas and his balanced view ran into vigorous resistance. But Aegidus Romanus defended him: 'There are people who are quickly inclined to describe as error statements by teachers through whom the Church is enlightened and faith illumined. They deceive themselves and besides, bring the faith into danger. The statements of those men who lead us on the ways of truth appeal to those who seek improvement in goodwill and freedom, and not to such as spread poison by slander. Let the way be barred to no one to think differently where he may do so without danger for the faith. And let pupils not be forced to hold to their teacher in every opinion he teaches, for our mind is not bound to any man, but only in obedience to Christ . . . And if someone holds a divergent opinion, people should not at once speak of error' (*Quaestio de gradibus formarum*; Venice, 1502, fol. 206, V).

Aegidius Romanus had to withdraw these words and sign the condemnation of Aquinas in order to be admitted as Master of Theology at the University of Paris.

I have just given a rapid and, I must admit, somewhat dry introduction on these two points. I now want to try to fill out this framework and depict the intellectual aspect of the personality of Aquinas in the light of the earliest accounts. I shall undertake this enquiry at three points: inner attitude towards the world, life of knowledge, and life of the will, in Aquinas.

The intellectual aspect of Thomas Aquinas. With Thomas doctrine and life formed an inner unity. He realized that great and attractive thing that I have called 'harmony' at the beginning of this chapter. What he taught he tried to put into practice in his life. For me that was the key to the understanding of his personality. His basic approach to reality I have recognized as a dialectical, balancing attitude: he subordinated human capabilities to an objective order and at the same time grew, in his subjectivity, in the power to *create* order. How did he realize this attitude in his own life?

Inward attitude towards the world. In his childhood Thomas adopted a withdrawn attitude, holding himself in the background. He let reality come to him. Of his childhood years in Monte Cassino it was reported that 'he was a child who did not talk much, but one who had begun to be thoughtfully silent' (ASS 658 D). This quality of his became more marked during his student days: 'He became more and more marvellously silent' (ASS 660 F), so that his fellow students called him 'the dumb ox' (ASS 661 A). Later, too, he remained a silent person: 'He answered one more in the soul than with words' (ASS 666 E). And 'One would have thought he passed his time more where his mind drew him than where he was staying in the body' (ASS 671 C). James de Cacatia says concisely of him: 'He was a lover of solitude' (ASS 704 B). William de Tocco characterizes him in this way: 'He was a humble man, despised earthly goods, and was very pure' (ASS 704 B).

I can fill out these abstract concepts with more content. Humble: it was most probably William de Tocco himself to whom Thomas told one of his visions. One evening

E

Thomas fell asleep in tears. In a dream a Brother who had died appeared to him and asked why he wept. Thomas replied: 'I am weeping because the burden of teaching has been given to me, for which my knowledge is by no means adequate' (ASS 663 A). He 'despised' earthly goods. One day the Brothers made an expedition. In the evening they were returning again to Paris. Among them was Thomas, at that time already a famous professor. His brethren said to him, 'Master, look, how beautiful the city of Paris is. Would you like to be Lord of this city?' Thomas replied, 'If this city were mine I should no longer be able to devote myself to the study of divine things, because of the cares of government' (ASS 671 A). And, very pure. I do not want to insist here on this feature in the picture of Aquinas' character. But perhaps I should at least relate what those who knew him particularly well said of him. Brother Albert de Brixia once 'met' St Augustine in a vision. I do not mean to enlarge on the subject of the authenticity of the vision, or of visions in general, nor to investigate whether or how apparitions occur. The important point for me is simply what opinion prevailed among the contemporaries of Thomas Aquinas. In short, Augustine, asked about Thomas Aquinas, replied, 'In glory he is equal to me, with the exception that he surpasses me in chastity' (ASS 706 E).

These few details are already enough to show how the personality of Aquinas embodied the first polarity in his doctrinal attitude: in his stance towards the world Thomas submitted to an order of things and demands independent of himself.

On the other hand, however, this freely chosen subordination of his subjective life to objective reality made it possible for him to develop a subjectivity of such richness that it mastered and formed things in a sovereign manner and style. I will mention here, for example, his method of working—his references to sources are by no means mechanical. He was no eclectic and did not range thoughts alongside each other. In his work he was very self-sufficient. Although he was familiar with what other thinkers before him had said, he never lost sight of his own goal : 'In the study of philosophy the most important thing is not to know what others have already thought but what is the truth of things' (*De coelo et mundo*, 1 : 22).

I find also that he was never disturbed in the creative projection of his thoughts by struggles with himself: 'The burden of the body was never able to disturb the lofty flight of his spirit, directed increasingly towards the divine' (ASS 667 D). 'The spirit seemed to be freed from his body' (ASS 664 B). William de Tocco gives another piece of important evidence here. He says that he had 'heard the general confession of Aquinas before his death. His whole life consisted in prayer, in contemplation, in lectures, disputations, writing and dictating' (ASS 704 B). What strenuous and sovereign spiritual activity is indicated by these simple words. The subjectivity of Thomas Aquinas perfectly mastered the objective circumstances, formed them and gave them permanence.

If I now sum up here these two polarities, there emerges a picture of Thomas Aquinas that is very highly nuanced, and this applies also to the Christian thinker as such. The Christian thinker is obliged to subordinate himself to norms proceeding from the object, as it were to sacrifice himself to them. But, in this sacrifice of his subjectivity, his 'ego' becomes ever richer, ever renewed, until he himself develops into a creator of new objectivity. In this he grows further as a subject is renewed. Aurelius Augustinus had already defined this subtle dialectic: 'To grow in renewal and be renewed in growth' (*Novatus crescere et crescendo novari*, in Psalm 131 : 1).

The life of knowledge. From the original documents I take it, on the one hand, that Thomas Aquinas was a contemplative person not only in his doctrine, but in his daily life. John of Naples testifies at the very beginning of his account: 'He was a man of exemplary contemplation' (ASS 699 F). An unknown member of the Order, from Fossanuova, could say of him only that he was 'carried away among heavenly things' (ASS 700 C). Peter de Sancto Felice reported that even at meals Thomas was so full of thought that 'one could have taken everything that stood before him away without his noticing' (ASS 698 E). There is reference to his 'unceasingly "concentrated" mind' (ASS 667 D).

Two events are generally known and illustrate excellently his intellectual dedication. St Louis, King of France, had often heard of Thomas Aquinas, and wanted to make his acquaintance. So he invited him to dine at his table. Aquinas, however, was in the middle of work on his *Summa Theologica*, and politely declined the invitation. The King then applied to the Prior. Thomas, in obedience to the Prior, went to dine with the King. But his mind remained on his work. The splendid meal began, and Thomas ate at the King's side. However, the whole room was uneasy. Everyone was watching Thomas

Aquinas. He sat there, completely sunk in thought, without exchanging a word with the King. Suddenly Thomas struck the table and said, 'Now I have the proof to smash the Manichaean heresy'. The Prior, who was also at the meal, went up to Thomas and 'grasped him rather vigorously by the cowl, and roused him from his absent-mindedness with the words "Master, remember that you are now sitting at the table of the King of France"' (ASS 671 C–D).

On another occasion a Cardinal visited the friary, to see Thomas. He was brought before the Cardinal in front of the whole community. But he was so much sunk in thought that he said nothing. Everyone waited for a sign of life. The Cardinal began to think Thomas was mad. This time, too, the Prior went up to him (obviously this was his method) and shook him a little by the cowl, whereupon Thomas at once came to himself, and greeted the Cardinal with great charm (ASS 671 E).

At the end of his life—the great *Summa Theologica* was still not finished—Thomas ceased to write: 'Such things were revealed to me that I regarded everything I had written until now as nothing, or as only a little' (ASS 672 D). Then comes his famous saying, 'I hope to God that as the end of my teaching has come, so the end of my life will soon come too' (ASS 672 E).

I see here again the first pole of his personality—total dedication to objective reality and the subordination of his person to knowledge.

At the same time, indeed in the same breath, he realized the other aspect of the polarity. His person became the measure of objective knowledge. On the one hand it was said of him that he was 'wonderfully contemplative', but at once it was added that 'his whole life was filled with work' (ASS 677 D). He seemed to be so sure in his judgment that 'during his whole life he changed little in his teaching, either in his lectures or in his writings' (ASS 670 D). It is further recorded that 'he once remarked in a friendly conversation . . . that he had never read a book that he had not understood with the help of the Holy Spirit' (ASS 670 D). Aegidius Romanus reproached the Dominicans that 'they would hide the writings of Thomas Aquinas from others, so that they themselves might appear knowledgeable and intelligent' (ASS 713 A). The older brothers recounted how astonished they were to see how Thomas Aquinas in so short a time (there were only twenty years between his becoming 'Magister' and his death) 'had been able to produce so much that was new' (ASS 664 A).

In his Foreword to the *Summa Theologica* we read: 'Since the teacher of Catholic truth should not instruct only those who are advanced, but his office is also to teach beginners . . . in this work the goal we have set before us is to present the content of the Christian religion in a manner that corresponds to the formation of beginners' (*S.Th.*, Prologue). When we stand before the grandiose architecture of the *Summa* and read this introduction, we are seized with astonishment at the creative power of Thomas Aquinas, who intended to write all this for beginners.

Here again I discover the tension already depicted between objective and subjective. In his life of knowledge Thomas gave himself over completely to the objective data, and as it were soaked them up. In this way his intellect grew to such a stature that it was itself able to become a creative source of objective values.

Finally I should like to go briefly into his *life of will*. One cannot understand Thomas Aquinas' life of the will apart from the spirit of the Western monastic fathers. The spirit of mildness, calm and peace he acquired early, in the Benedictine centre of spiritual life in Monte Cassino. It was remarked of him, 'Reason and feeling became one in him (ASS 668 C). 'He never began to work, without first having prayed' (ASS 704 B). 'On concluding his work, or at a difficult passage, he again sought refuge in prayer' (ASS 704 B).

There is a story of Thomas at the castle of Montesangiovanni, where his relations locked him up. The chronicle relates that they sent to him a 'very beautiful girl', to tempt him. The young Thomas leapt up, snatched a burning brand out of the fireplace, and chased the girl out with it. Then he traced a cross on the wall with the brand, knelt down and prayed God for the grace of perfect purity for his whole life. It is said that God then sent him two angels who put round him a 'girdle of chastity' (ASS 659 F–660 B). At any rate his confessor testifies that his last confession was 'like the confession of a five-year-old child' (ASS 667 A).

Less well-known, but very characteristic of his ready sacrifice of his own will, is the following story: A young lay Brother came into the community at Paris. The Prior sent him to do the shopping, and told him to take with him the first Brother he met. Aquinas was accustomed to walk up and down across the cloister when he came to a difficult question. The Brother came by, saw Thomas, and immediately said to him, 'Good brother, the Prior orders that you come with me.' For the whole day Thomas trailed around behind the lay brother, carrying a sack full of purchases. The secretaries waited in vain, and the lecture hall too. All over the town people laughed at the Dominicans for making the famous Professor carry a sack. When they came back and the brothers rushed up to them, Thomas replied, 'All religion is perfected in obedience' (ASS 666 C–D).

Thomas took the poverty of the Order so seriously that he wrote part of the *Summa contra Gentiles* on little scraps of paper, as he happened to have no other paper (ASS 706 C). With him all this was simply the expression of a deep commitment to Christ. In the acts of his canonization we read that Aquinas had just finished a part of the *Summa Theologica*, on the passion and resurrection of Christ, when Christ appeared to him: 'Thomas, you have written well of me. What do you want from me as reward?' Aquinas answered simply, 'Nothing but you yourself, Lord' (ASS 669 B).

At the same time this mild, good-humoured and humble man could be extraordinarily down-to-earth. In the acts of canonization we find repeatedly with what accuracy and persistence he fought against heresies, or even mere philosophical errors, for example those of Averroes and his successors (cf. ASS 664–665 E).

Contemplation was of real 'use' to him, in the ordinary sense of the word. In his view the highest stage of life in the Order was to pass on to others what has been seen in prayer (*S.Th.*, II–II q. 118, a. 6, corp.). The return to earthly things should occur 'from out of the fulness of contemplation'.

Out of love he subordinated himself to all that was real, and thereby himself grew to become a force creating reality. In the end his life broke against this tension. He had not yet finished his *Summa Theologica* when one day he stopped dictating. His mass lasted a long time. Finally Aquinas went to his cell. Brother Raynaldus reports: 'After this mass he wrote no more, nor did he dictate' (ASS 711 C). He was repeatedly pressed to do so, but he always answered, 'Raynaldus, I can't any more.' He gave the reason: 'I have seen such things in comparison with which all that I have written seems to me like straw' (ASS 711 D).

A general Council had been called for 1 May 1274 at Lyons. At the wish of the Pope Aquinas travelled there. On the way he became seriously ill and asked his companions to take him to the Cistercian monastery of Fossanuova. Despite the best treatment his strength failed. He tried, in broken sentences, to comment on the Song of Songs for the members of the Order. He was given communion, and then extreme unction. The following morning, 7 March, a Wednesday, he gave up his soul. Aquinas is a supreme example of a man whose life and teaching were one.

Dante and vision

Dante and vision

I want now to present the Christian image of man in its perfected form, but at the same time to 'practise vision', or learn it afresh. This 'seeing things with Christian eyes' is something I look upon as still almost unexplored territory. It is certainly a fundamental task. Contemplation is not all passive but at times a strenuous exploration, a self-commitment that seeks to be acknowledged. Seeing brings with it the power to see. It contains attitudes of vocation and self-discovery, of listening and inwardness, in a word the capacity for encounter.

I once asked Romano Guardini, my revered teacher, what phenomenology really was. He answered, in his wonderfully simple way: 'Eyes open and mouth shut.' By this he meant, I think, that you must let objects work upon you for a time, and guard against immediately naming them, 'ticking them off', cataloguing them. Fundamentally you don't want to 'get anything out of' contemplation of the word, or want to 'achieve' anything by it. You stand first of all before the object, in purity of vision, in an initial, virgin state of perception. There what some thinkers call the 'joint vision of the furthest areas of knowledge' can happen. At a single glance you survey the most varied objects in the world. You no longer distinguish. Only thus can you uncover and 'see' in them a mysterious interconnexion, which you can often only struggle to express. That is why Guardini called most of his writings 'experiments' or 'interpretations'.

Hans Urs von Balthasar wrote about Guardini in another connexion and entitled the passage 'Co-vision': 'In the ranks of historians of the mind there are some of particular distinction who ask deeper and more searching questions than the others, and so touch on deeper sources in the listener who is called to a decision. In the great Monographs containing his dialogues Guardini deliberately chose figures . . . who are not the creators of massive systems in philosophy or theology (it is a little different with the poets) but provide, as it were, areas of openness where basic questions break through, windows spring open, lights flash out, places where the love of questioning thrusts its way upwards but—as ever—does not turn away from any light from above; places where historical periods break off and pass on to something new, where what is questionable and what is hopeful both appear, where bridge-building becomes possible. Places where only a total commitment will avail—of life and thought as one.'

In this sense I regard 'vision' as a great virtue in a thinker and as an uncovenanted gift. Why this concern for vision? In a way, our whole life is involved in it. Man is the centre-point of the world, the axis and fulcrum of a universal aspiration of the world. In us the streams of the 'will to life' of the universe converge and struggle through towards God, the ultimate object of vision. Only in our pure future, when the reality of our being, and with it the being of the whole world, finds itself in the vision of God, only then will we encounter our final form of existence.

Thus the 'perfected man' and his inner form are not available but detectable only by visionary perception. There was a man of the Middle Ages who knew how to speak strikingly to us about this—Dante Alighieri. I should even assert that there were two 'wonders' of the Middle Ages: one was the Gothic cathedrals of France, the other Dante's *Divina Commedia*.

The first idea for Dante Alighieri's greatest work no doubt arose from his resolve to glorify his love, his unconsummated devotion to a woman, Beatrice. Dante devoted a book, *La Vita Nuova*, 'New Life', to his encounter with her: 'The lights of heaven had almost completed their ninth revolution since my birth when there appeared before my eyes the noble mistress of my soul, named Beatrice by those who sought a mortal name for her.'

Beatrice died young and Dante's love remained for ever unfulfilled. It was a childhood love, which so dominated Dante's young life that it became an image of the love of God. So pure and unclouded was this love that it drew forth some of the most beautiful verses ever composed in our Western hemisphere. Dante waited for a long time before he could express all that he felt for this little creature behind whom, for him, shone the countenance of the Creator. The book ends with these words: 'After this Sonnet, I had a vision. In it I saw things that aroused in me the longing to fall silent, to say no more of my beloved until I could do it more worthily . . . And may it please the Lord of goodness that my soul be raised to see the glory that Beatrice now sees revealed, the face of him who is blessed for all eternity.'

The *Vita Nuova* belongs, with Plato's *Phaedo*, Augustine's *Confessions* and Pascal's *Pensées*, among the books

that hold an indestructible power of life. What raises
these books into the sphere of the immortals is their
intensity of vision and greatness of experience. Dante's
Vita Nuova describes only a meeting with a child. In
later years this meeting was repeated, with a truth and
fervour that reveals to anyone who is open to it how the
love of one person can become the measure of true life
and creativity.

The world of the *Divina Commedia* is an 'other-
worldly' universe: Hell, Purgatory, Heaven. Dante was
born more than seven hundred years ago, in May 1265,
in Florence. He died in September 1321, in exile in
Ravenna. From his twentieth year onwards he produced
works so various that it is hard to believe they sprang
from the mind of a single man. But everything Dante
wrote before the *Commedia* was taken up into the
mighty world of this creation. Dante once called his poem
'il sacro poema, al quale ha posta mano e cielo e terra':

> The sacred poem, that hath made
> Both heaven and earth copartners in its toil*

The people whom the poem is about are dead. But
Dante's voice gives them living words. They have the
sorrows, passions and hopes of living people. It is true,
as has been said, the world of the *Commedia* is
intended to be other-worldly, yet somehow formulated in
an earthly, even earthy manner. Dante had an amazing
poetic gift for visualizing a whole teeming world,
forming it, and making it centre from every side on the
main idea of the poem.

* All quotations from the *Commedia Divina* are from Cary's
version.

This main idea is, in brief, as follows: Human life has departed from God. But the return home is entrusted to man. Beyond all the misfortune of the falling away from God lies the saving hope of a return to God. Man—and he alone—had the existential movement of migration towards self-realization and a growing intensification of being, as being with the other. Human nature is born to ascend. It is born:

> at last to form
> the winged insect, imp'd with angel plumes

Dante's life as a poet seems like something God-given, surounded by a halo of grace: 'God took me up into his grace.'

> O grace . . . that gavest
> Boldness to fix so earnestly my ken
> On the everlasting splendour . . .

Woven into a grandiose picture of his times, Dante's memory of the love of his youth became the experience of God's goodness, and the vision of the profundity of the Trinity. Great poets seem to lie under a curious compulsion to seize hold of the whole polarity of human existence, both its dark and light sides. In the *Commedia* what is ugly, mean and distorted is given shape as well as what is beautiful, noble and enlightened. In the shifting contrast of darkness and light everything thinkable in human degradation and despair makes its appearance, but also ultimate perfection with God in heaven.

Between the two realms lies the *Purgatorio*, a realm of fulfilment in expectation, in which the wind already blows freely and the light shines clear. It is a realm of peace, coming from God's mercy. A God who bends in forgiveness over those who were unjust but whose souls lament over the faults they have committed. The hope of coming soon to God fills them with consolation. The longing of the human soul rises freely and untrammelled up to God. People sing, pray for grace, rejoice. They are all seized with a supernatural joy when one of them is allowed to ascend to God.

Dante's *Purgatorio* is a song of restrained tenderness. Even his powerful language is moderated in these cantos. Perhaps for this reason, precisely this part of the *Commedia*, otherwise in ideas and in an overall human sense the most beautiful, is so little regarded by students of literature. There arises, in yearning for goodness and beauty, something final and lasting, out of man's broken existence. All the language and imagery are fitted and subordinated to this quiet process of transition to finality. The coming of heaven, the most essential thing in human life, is seen there: the man who is broken and dependent on the mercy of God, but yet is filled with hope and joy. In what consists Dante's insight into this essence of our being? How is man perfected? What testing must be endured in order to be completely cleansed? What ultimately matters in our life?

According to Dante, the essential man develops when his life no longer sets obstacles to the grace and friendship of God, and he is willing to be made totally happy by God.

The poem begins timidly, like every first resolve for God: 'Era già l'ora che volge il disio':

Now was the hour that wakens fond desire . . .
The pilgrim newly on his road with love
Thrills, if he hear the vesper bell from far,
That seems to mourn for the expiring day:
When I . . .
Began, with wonder
From those spirits to mark
One risen from its seat . . .
Both palms it join'd and raised
. . . as telling God
'I care for nought beside'.

All eyes shine with longing:

I saw that gentle band silently next
Look up, as if in expectation held,
Pale and in lowly guise.

In these men the course of fate is no longer held back.
The process of becoming fully human is depicted in the
Purgatorio as an 'ascent to God' in which men have
gradually to climb up seven storeys or circuits of a
mountain, before they come to the top, whence they can
enter straight into heaven. Thus human existence is
thought of as an upward striving.

In the fire of purgatory the abyss of one's own being
has to be surmounted. This is the purification. But the
higher one reaches, the easier the climb becomes, as one
becomes ever more free from burdens. Dante has crossed
the gate of the *Purgatorio* with his companion, Virgil.
With that, something final happened, symbolized in the
image of the gate closing:

> When we had past the threshold of the gate . . .
> I heard its closing sound.

Both are now separated from the remainder of mankind living outside their proper being. A new condition is opened to them, the humanization of man. In this Dante conceives an astonishing existential philosophy of human self-realization. The introductory step leading to a truly human life is, for Dante:

First of all, humility. On the first storey, in the circle of the proud, Dante can make out hardly any human form, only beings so bent as to be 'blinded'. They cannot look up, only at the ground. Their vision has not yet been brought into living action. 'Instructor,' Dante cries out, 'what I see . . . bears no trace of human semblance.' Virgil replies to his frightened cry:

> Beneath their heavy terms
> Of torment stoop they . . .
> Like the untimely embryon of a worm
> Those spirits went beneath a weight like that
> We sometimes feel in dreams.

Even the most patient of them complains, 'Più non posso' —'I can endure no more'.

A man when and in so far as he wants to be a man, must think himself into what is ever greater, indeed into the impossible. He cannot ascend totally as he is, with what he has already realized in his life. But out of this straining towards greatness an evil division can arise. The man feels himself unfulfilled. A disgust at his own being, a protest against himself, arises in his consciousness. Eventually the man 'lies' to himself about what he really is. He is no longer content to be as he has become, indeed no longer willing to be at all. Then the essential question arises for him: Does God really know what he is expecting of us when he wants us to accept ourselves, to endure ourselves, to bear with our own insufficiencies and fallibility? But the power in which we master ourselves and the life entrusted to us, in which we and with us the life won by love around us can thrive, is humility.

It is not weakness. It is understanding of what it means that I have only this and nothing else. I must not waste my life by constantly saying 'I' and again 'I'. Humility means that a man resolves to take God's hand with trust in his guidance; that he becomes little with the little ones, honours the old, shows courtesy to women, keeps unpleasantness from others, takes the weak under the protection of his strength, moderates the movements of inner violence, lightens life for others, so that no evil befalls them.

A man who does not know how to humble himself, who loses respect for the little ones out of noisy self-awareness, becomes himself inwardly small and impoverished. Often a man is afraid to give his fundamental attitude to life its right name: humility. Or more simply, tenderness and courtesy towards creatures. God however 'behaves' in this way towards us: 'Behold, I stand at the door and knock' (Rev. 3:20). Humility is where God's heart is revealed to us, in Christ. Whenever a man has only himself in view he bars the way to his own self-realization, forgets his own greatness. Therefore he must become humble. Not as a punishment, but as a starting-point for all self-realization, because his own way to greatness prescribes it:

O powers of man! how vain your glory, nipt
E'en in its height of verdure.

Secondly: magnanimity. In the purgatory of the envious
Dante and Virgil are not met with cries, or groans of
bitterness, but only with lamentation and blindness. The
penitents lean like blind beggars against the wall of rock.
Dante feels sympathy for them and speaks to them with
exquisite courtesy. The poetry is filled with the yearning
of the blinded souls and the tender feeling of the poet.

Envy is that fault in human character that cannot
recognize the beauty and uniqueness of the other, and
denies them honour. In order to approach God, who is
total beauty and uniqueness, this attitude must be broken
from within. Envy can no longer see. The eyes are
inwardly 'nailed down'.

Of sackcloth vile
Their covering seemed . . . and all lean'd
Against the cliff. E'en thus the blind and poor,
Near the confessionals, to crave an alms,
Stand, each with his head upon his fellow's sunk . . .
It were a wrong, methought, to pass . . .

Cantos 13–14 tell us of the fate of human envy:

'Through the orbs of all
A thread of wire, impressing, knits them up . . . their
cheeks
Bathing devout with penitential tears

Dante's soul was moved by the sight:

Pity for your sakes hath wrung my heart

These men could not even look upon their own perfection:

Heaven calls . . .
With everlasting beauties. Yet your eyes
Turn with fond doting still upon the earth.

Heaven itself strives for man. And he does not even notice it. What a tragedy of human blindness! Much evil comes from envy. One is poor and sees another richly supplied. Everyone feels in some respect that another possesses what he himself painfully lacks. But the man who cannot come to terms with the fact, who lets himself be embittered by it, who grudges another what he has, he will poison his own life. There rises up within him a hostility towards life itself.

Magnanimity, however, is capable of looking beyond itself, can grant the other what oneself perhaps bitterly lacks, and can perhaps even rejoice in the other's greatness and beauty. God has given into men's hands their life in this world. Our magnanimity allows others to be what they are—to live according to their nature, and to be greater than ourselves. Magnanimity lets the other be free, for that other must become great enough to be an image of God. Magnanimity arouses in us the desire for the other to receive the greatest possible satisfaction, and every happiness that can accrue to him.

In the same way magnanimity does not expect the other to subject himself to what *we* have. The generous man has the will to become the image of divine goodness, to wish for every creature its own perfection. Magnanimity also has the power of attracting other men to God: 'Enter into the joy of your master' (Mt. 25:21).

To wish this for all men—that is real magnanimity. Again the point is that we have to atone for our envy not as a punishment, but in order that we may be able to know God's greatness, so that our heart may become open to God. From then on, from this cheerful selflessness which is what magnanimity means, our way leads to God through what Dante describes in the fifteenth to seventeenth cantos of the *Purgatorio*.

Thirdly: mildness. Dante sees in the picture of the proto-martyr, Stephen, the realization of true human nature:

> After that I saw
> A multitude, in fury burning, slay
> With stones a stripling youth, and shout amain
> 'Destroy, destroy'; and him I saw, who bow'd
> Heavy with death unto the ground, yet made
> His eyes, unfolded upward, gates to heaven,
> Praying forgiveness of the Almighty Sire,
> Amidst that cruel conflict, on his foes.

An angel appears directly to Dante:

> I perceived
> Near me as 'twere the waving of a wing,
> That fann'd my face, and whisper'd 'Blessed they,
> The peacemakers: they know not evil wrath'.

What can a man bring about in another by his own will? His ill-will can destroy men. His fear can poison many. His desire can overpower. A man should test himself, whether he does such things. Jesus always seeks out men and brings them to God. He is concerned with the outcast and dishonoured, those who are despised and

whom no one helps in their need. He seeks what was
lost. He has spoken to all. He never desired men's
humiliation. That was the 'folly' of Jesus—to call the poor
and outcast to himself. It was a creative love that prevailed in Jesus. God's first action upon the things of this
world is that he says to them, Be!—Be your own self. God's
creative mildness creates the sphere in which we live. A
decent man therefore feels called upon to respect all that
is defenceless. He pauses before helplessness, is touched
by the presence of a painful fate, and abandons himself
to it.

Today we need people who dare to be mild. Who do
not answer evil with evil. Who are a hope for others.
People who find words of forgiveness for others. Thus
mildness is more than a little 'feeling'. It is a duty. God
wants us to carry on our lives as part of the life of
Christ, to enter into the fulfilment of Christ's purpose,
in an attitude of quiet regard for all life, of love for
life.

> The soul . . .
> Artless, and as ignorant of aught,
> Save that her Maker being one who dwells
> With gladness ever, willingly she turns
> To whate'er yields her joy.

And so, according to Dante, there remains for all
creation the hope that one day mildness will rule over
all being:

> All from self-hatred are secure; and since
> No being can be thought to exist apart,
> And independent of the first, a bar
> Of equal force restrains from hating that.

A man should therefore never so lose the 'courage to be' that he feels completely thrown back upon himself. The eighteenth canto of the *Purgatorio* is dedicated to this 'courage to live'. Its message is concentrated in the demand for

Fourthly: joy. Joy in being should always be the atmosphere of a Christian life. Inner weariness or indifference, upon which Dante here declares war, are basically cold and lasting hatred against what is alive in the world and in one's own being. For the future of man and of all that is beautiful and a source of happiness in the world, man must awaken from his lethargy, must 'pull himself together'.

It has to be himself that is involved, as is everyone and everything. If a man feels that he cannot summon any sympathy or enthusiasm either for himself or for anyone or anything else, then he must consider that what is involved is necessarily something sacred, the sanctification of his feeling for his own self.

Dante seems to be saying to such a man: If you are still alive, rouse up more life in yourself. If you are sleeping, wake up. If you are dead, arise from the dead. Seek out the best, most beautiful memories in your past life, now perhaps extinguished! Take your longing, your prayer, your love and throw all that in the scale of life and joy! Of all the stupidities with which the devil surrounds us one is the most destructive: 'Life is boring'. The soul of man is created for divine joy.

If you love boredom, then you are related to nothingness. But if you love life, if you love happiness, if you love love, then you are on your way to God. The devil is the prince of disgust. God by contrast is the Lord of joy.

It is true that often all seems to have turned to disgust in us. All 'impressions' little by little die away. But there are people—God has created them so and given us them as an example in our lives—for whom joy, bravery, pleasure in existence and honour, are all one. Such a man feels everywhere the challenge of life and feels obliged to take it up. He may not be particularly strong physically. Perhaps he is liable to pain and sensitive to blows and setbacks from without and within. Nonetheless, he stands firm, and goes quietly onwards. He meets events without fear. Thus the inner nobility of the man becomes clear. And also, of course, his predestination to the difficulties of life, his call to bear these difficulties, in order to maintain joy in the world.

It would perhaps be appropriate to consider Christ's attitude towards life, to let it influence your spirit. I have often realized what courage to live, what inner harmony he brought to bear upon his fate, and what joy burned in his heart. He truly lived out the condition of the world, endured it all to the very end. I sense what that meant for him in the hour of Gethsemane. If you think of all this, you may shudder at the thought of what it meant there to 'face life with courage'. There it becomes clear what inner vitality means: the attitude that says ever again 'Nonetheless' and, despite everything that may seem senseless in life, takes up the struggle against sadness.

Trying to be a Christian means letting your mood be ruled by this attitude of Christ, even when you have every reason to be discouraged and despairing. If you could only sense the joy of Christ—that depth of cheerfulness and goodwill—then you would be cheerful your whole life long.

Dante describes the attitude of men who are striving toward God in the following way:

> ... Suddenly a multitude ...
> Rush'd on ...
> By eagerness impell'd of holy love.
> Soon they o'ertook us; with such swiftness moved
> The mighty crowd. Two spirits at their head
> Cried, weeping, 'Blessed Mary sought with haste the
>   hilly region ...'
> 'Oh, tarry not: away!'
> The others shouted, 'Let not time be lost
> Through slackness of affection. Hearty zeal
> To serve reanimates celestial grace.'

Dante had been 'musing in dreamy slumber; but not long Slumbered'.

Whence can this fine courage toward life flow in upon a man? Dante finds an answer that is deeply right, and very noteworthy for many of us today: from poverty. Hence the next requirement is:

Fifthly: generosity. If you want to get close to the 'God of all grace', you must be completely free in giving. Dante continues his ascent as if in a dream in the 'Purgatory of the Avaricious'. These are bound with their whole being to the earth:

> All downward lying prone and weeping sore,
> 'My soul hath cleaved to the dust,' I heard ...
> I was a soul in misery, alienate from God,
> And covetous of all earthly things ...
> Here justice holds us prison'd hand and foot.

Cantos 19 to 20 of the *Purgatorio* are the most grip-
ping and at the same time the most graceful in all Dante's
poetry. Dante makes it clear to us that man's happiness
does not consist in seizing everything for himself. Rather
the whole meaning of the gospel is contained in God's
words to us: 'He who abides in love abides in God,
and God abides in him' (1 John 4 : 16).

Love is the spirit of God. We can never grasp this
truth concretely and really enough. In our life it is
important above all that God's love becomes 'real' in us,
active and effective. Therefore it is said, quite soberly,
in the first letter of John: 'But if any one has the world's
goods, and sees his brother in need, yet closes his heart
against him, how does God's love abide in him?' (1 John
3 : 17). The man who is not a free giver is not born of
God, is not of God's kind.

The claims of such a love are strict. A man must learn
that the essence of the matter is not that we should pro-
mote ourselves and our interests in the world, but that
our neighbour at any time, the person who is by me, can
find in me room to live, that he can breathe freely and
prosper, that he can at last be 'himself'. This 'spirituality
of a new man' consists in the conviction that a man can
'sanctify' his brother, that he must let himself become
powerful in the selflessness of his love. In order to do
this—Dante tells us in cantos 21–4 of the *Purgatorio*—
a man must live in the manner that he calls:

Sixthly: self-mastery. Basically self-mastery means
modesty of spirit. I can not really believe that a man can of
his nature strive for evil and impurity. The force of good
seems to rule him completely. And so hate will never be
able completely to conquer love. However many-sided evil

may be, it will never be able to devour the good in us. To 'master' oneself for good is the attitude in which creation strives in us towards its completion, becomes goodness in us.

How does the spiritual life of such a man appear? To put it more correctly, how must it appear if it is to correspond completely to our human and Christian calling? God does not want of us any 'renunciation of the world' but a 'sacrifice in the world' for men, and thus in fact for God. We only need to take the word 'self-mastery' literally. Then it means nothing other than 'mastery over oneself', an uncompromising fulfilment of all that is meant by love and self-lessness. The more intensely a man experiences life—in his suffering and in his happiness—the more undivided he will want to be, because this life has so great a need of love. The greatest good a man can do to the world and his fellow men is surely this: to live without reserve and without *arrière pensée*, to be totally available to others.

'God give you peace, my brethren'—thus runs God's call to our humanity. Peace however can be granted only by a man whose breast burns with love. In order to be worthy of this attitude Dante invites us to go again through the fire of purification, to become all sacrifice. This means:

Seventhly: purity. The basic Christian attitude to life means to give up, to renounce everything (to say farewell to every resting place) that does not help us in the service of a higher life. Purity seeks only that we be ready unreservedly for love, for the Other: not regarding self, selfless, life giving. Dante speaks to us of this attitude in the closing cantos of the *Purgatorio* (cantos 25–7). There those are declared holy who are pure of heart. But purity does not mean only being free from disturbances of the senses, but a total inward purity, goodness of will before God and man.

Christ says that such a disposition will 'see' God. To know God is not a matter of mere understanding, but of a living gaze. If this gaze is clear, if the eye is pure; then the heart will also be pure, for the source of human vision lies in the heart. To know God it does not help much simply to strain the understanding. The heart must be purified. What does this mean?

Our spirit becomes 'impure' when it goes wrong, when it misunderstands concepts, when it confuses images: that is to say, when it no longer has the will to see what is; when it defiles the meaning of things and of existence, takes from them their nobility, by word and deed; when it no longer sees the honour of truth as its own. On this there is much more to be said here, and especially in the world of today. For a man can fall sick through impurity —a quite different sickness from that resulting from accident or infection. The mind can become sick in its relationship to truth: if it dispenses with truth as such, or falls away from it, or subordinates it to some other goal, or obscures it.

The guarantee of purity of mind is adoration of God. So long as a man adores God, so long as he bows to him, he remains inwardly sound and well. Man as he is, the most vulnerable and easily misled of creatures, needs protection. There must be something in which the heart of man is constantly renewed, his mind cleansed, his vision cleared. Adoration is precisely this:

There is nothing more important for a man than that

he should learn to bow down in his whole inward being before God, make way for him, for the infinity he has to gain; that he should accept inwardly that God is worthy of adoration without end or reservation; that he should kneel down and make himself aware that God is and reigns, that he is worthy to possess all power; that he is worthy to be God.

Perhaps we can find a great happiness in the thought that God is worthy to be God! Saints have 'burned' with love because of it. The heart often needs no words, but simply bows down, filled with love. It can also happen that we are dumb and resistant. Then it is already something if we set ourselves in God's presence, and for a while are 'there' with him. Such moments will work their way deep into our life, and render it inwardly fruitful.

> Now was the sun so station'd, as when first
> His early radiance quivers on the heights . . .
> . . . when the angel of God
> Appear'd before us. Joy was in his vision . . .
> . . . 'Blessed are the pure
> In heart', he sang . . . and 'Come', we heard,
> 'Come, blessed of my Father.' Such the sounds
> That hail'd us from within a light . . .
> 'Expect no more
> Sanction of warning voice or sign from me,
> Free of thy own arbitrement to chuse,
> Discreet, judicious. To distrust thy sense
> Were henceforth error.
> I invest thee then
> With crown and mitre, sovereign o'er thyself.'

A humble man, dedicated to magnanimity, mild, living in joy, generous, pure, master of himself! I must ask my Lord that he grant me the grace to sense ever more clearly in my life this marvellous newness, that with him has broken into our existence, and to help it break through whenever I am able. It is men like that who represent God's presence in the world. For this is needed above all holiness of action.

A man does not become holy in the first instance by being a 'specialist in divine things' but by selfless service to his neighbour in daily life: to the neighbour who before could only say, 'I have no one!'

One who goes out and looks for a poor man to whom no one else will listen, such a person, be he Christian or pagan, will hear the words of Christ, 'You are blessed. For you I have prepared a kingdom since the beginning of the world. You were a Christian.'

Augustine and appropriation

Augustine and appropriation

If you are to think with your whole being, then you have to enter into the kind of inner relation with the truth you're investigating that makes possible a real 'appropriation'. But for that kind of 'conversion' or 'taking over' you need meditation, inner peace, and probably a lot of prayer. It is important, too, to ask yourself such necessary questions as: 'If this statement is true, how can I go on living as I have until now?' 'How can I act out this truth?' 'What must become different in my life?' 'What conclusions for my own life must I draw from this insight?' The radical, existential questions are the first to come to mind.

The language of decision and resolution is the only one in which God approaches a Christian (even in thought). You can't simply take a truth for an outing, and chat with it under a tree, and then go home when its time comes. Truth itself is an entrance, and one from which there's no return. Any other way of thinking, any other attitude, would be dishonest, and thus unchristian. There is only this one kind of thinking 'in encounter', that can endure on earth. Genuine thinking wells up from within, and its truth can be guaranteed only by a man who is seized by it.

In these pages I have often tried to reach back in time to when I was first gripped by ideas. Far, far back. What happened to Ernst Wiechert has often happened to me and still does. Commenting on his autobiographical writings, he says: 'Sometimes, when I lecture in big cities, and especially abroad, I look along the gangway leading from my desk through the audience to the end of the hall. And then suddenly before my eyes it becomes even longer, like an endless road, running between dark bushes to the edges of the earth. And there, at the back, where the sides run together, I see standing—myself, as I once was: a child, barefoot, shepherd's staff in hand, setting out with his flock to conquer his world.'

It is part of the working of divine grace to pick out an individual and to care for him as if only this individual existed. 'O you God omnipotent, you care for every one of us, as if you cared for him only' (*Conf.,* 3, 11:19). (All quotations from the *Confessions* are from Pusey's translation—adapted.) For this saying, I must be eternally grateful to Aurelius Augustinus, and his *Confessions.*

From the beginning the inner character of the great African acted upon me like that of a brother or a friend. For me Augustine was never a creature of a special kind or alien personality. This is probably because he experienced human life in its most earthly forms. But wretchedness, weakness, doubts and fears could not stop his ardent search for God. Everywhere he sought God. His long wandering took him along all roads, ways and paths, all the small obscure back streets of our existence. His life, with its dramatic upheavals, errors and high points, was dominated by God. In it he was a man pursued by God: 'And you sent your hand from above, and drew my soul out of that profound darkness' (*Conf.,* 3, 11:19). 'You were close on the steps of your fugitives' (*Conf.,*

4, 11 : 7). 'By inward goads you roused me, so that I should be ill at ease, until you were manifest to my inward sight' (*Conf.*, 7, 8 : 12). And then the imperishable words: 'For you made us for yourself, and our heart is restless, until it reposes in you' (*Conf.*, 1, 1 : 1).

Man is released by God into his real being. He is set free to stand in his own centre and walk with his own gait. And yet he is not yet complete in himself. The form of his existence is that of an arch thrown out to him whom he encounters. Man has only finally found himself, brought himself to his completed form, when he has found his way to the close, direct 'you' or 'thou' in which God has placed himself before men.

The law of man's existence is the inner disquiet of his concentrated being (his heart). This disquiet is a mark of God's presence in human existence, and evidence of his power over the human heart. How true this experience is, and of what range, for the understanding of my own life, but also for the basic experiences of all human life.

I have felt, muffled and obscure, these living experiences within myself. Then came Augustine, and in his crystal-clear formulation it all turned into eternally valid knowledge. Where did he get this power of penetration from?

Augustine's life was concerned everywhere and always with love and yet more love. Truth, too, was for him an object of love, something that cannot be reached through theoretic reasoning, something that satisfies not only the mind, but also warms the heart. It is mildness, beauty, tenderness, satisfaction. God is present to man as the ground and origin of love: 'Blessed whosoever loves you, and his friend in you, and his enemy for you. For he alone loses none dear to him, to whom all are dear in Him who cannot be lost' (*Conf.*, 4, 9:14).

Only this attitude to existence enabled Augustine to penetrate to the ultimate depth of reality, and grasp it in its totality. In the tenth chapter of the seventh book of the *Confessions* Augustine comes to a decisive understanding of what it means to be a human being: Man is that being who can see God in his own life, feel him and affirm him in a vital decision of the heart; the being who can experience God not only theoretically and in the abstract, but in the incarnate, living spirit.

God is light. He is known not in detached objectivity but out of one's own being, in the relationship of 'I' and 'you'. The unchanging light is truth, but such a truth that knowledge of it depends on love: 'Who knows the truth knows it, and who knows it knows eternity. It is love that knows it.' God is: '. . . understood as one understands with the heart'.

In the ultimate depth of his character man is the being who can cry out: 'O Truth you are Eternity! Love you are Truth! Eternity you are Love! You are my God, to you I sigh night and day' (*Conf.*, 7, 10:16).

Such insights presuppose an extraordinary sensibility. Augustine was filled with an intense, long-lasting emotionality. There too I feel for him increasingly as a friend and brother. I think of the severity of the psychic traumas that his childhood memories left with him (*Conf.*, 1, 9:14–15). As a bishop, at the age of seventy-two, he could still write in his *City of God*: 'Who would not draw back in horror, and prefer death, if he were offered a choice between death and a return to childhood . . .' (*Civ. Dei.*, 21:14).

This sensitivity of Augustine's was intensified by a prolonged introspection and dissection of his soul. He was shaken by the subtlest, least perceptible processes in the soul. The whole horizon of his sensibility was filled by God and his own soul: 'God and the soul—otherwise nothing' (*Soliloq*., 1, 2 : 7).

With exceptional powers of reflexion he grasped the deepest elements of life, in a drama played out between God and the soul: 'You, O Lord, turned me round towards myself, taking me from behind my back, where I had placed myself, unwilling to observe myself; and setting me before my face' (*Conf*., 8, 7 : 16).

Internal experiences could shake the whole being of this hot-blooded man. He says of his search: 'I sought anxiously . . . what were the pangs of my teeming heart? . . . those silent contritions of my soul . . . I roared out . . . the tumult of my soul . . . found I no resting place . . . my pride-swollen face closed up my eyes' (*Conf*., 7, 7 : 11). 'There remained a mute shrinking . . . my forehead, cheeks, eyes, colour, tone of voice, spoke my mind more than the words I uttered . . . the tumult of my breast hurried me . . . I was healthily distracted . . . I was troubled in spirit, most vehemently indignant' (*Conf*., 8, 7 : 18; 8, 9 : 19).

These are all only sentences thrown together, half-sentences with the sharpest outlines, stretched to breaking point and filled with intense emotion. I see here how Augustine was called to the way of total sacrifice of body and soul, and also what that meant for him: 'By my very soul will I ascend to him. I will pass beyond that power which unites me to my body' (*Conf*., 10, 7 : 11).

What is happening here—I see it clearly and fearfully —is a total claim upon a human being by God's grace, and a total commitment of the man to the truth of an absolute love.

Here, in the *Confessions*, Christian subjectivity appears for the first time. There is at work in Augustine a marvellous power of self-reflexion, still shattering today. You can feel in everything the breath of the abyss of human existence. No wonder Augustine felt himself very isolated. With him it was the solitude of greatness. This explains why he was so withdrawn and indeed shy. To give only two examples:

He tried repeatedly to speak to Ambrose of Milan. He went into the reception room, open to all, and found the Bishop alone, busy silently reading. Augustine hesitated a long time, and then went away. And this was repeated several times: 'Often when we had come (for no man was forbidden to enter, nor did he order any who came to be announced to him) . . . having long sat silent (for who dare intrude on one so intent?) we wanted to go' (*Conf.*, 6, 3 : 3).

Another incident testifies to his shyness. In the *Confessions* he describes the treatise *De Magistro* which he composed jointly with his sixteen-year-old son, Adeodatus (*Conf.*, 9, 6 : 14). In it he analyses with profundity the difficulty he feels when he has to make contact with another mind and understand it. But that very shyness was also the reason—and I can only confirm this curious finding from my own, often painful experiences—for an exceptionally great capacity for friendship, indeed a powerful force of temptation. The loyalty and sincerity of so many friendships throughout Augustine's life testify to the richness of his heart: pupils and followers who later, like himself, became monks and bishops. A dangerous gift besides : how many friends did Augustine draw into the wilderness of Manichaeism during the ten years of his error?

This sketchy portrayal of Augustine's personality would be incomplete if I didn't consider his serious defects of character. I am not thinking so much of his dissolute life and the concubinage in which he lived for sixteen years. That irregular love-affair was accompanied on both sides by a touching loyalty; it bore fruit in a fine son whose spiritual development was admirable. I rather praise the reserve and sincerity of this relationship, which Augustine's mother, Monica, broke up with a hardness that was as injurious perhaps as it was devout and proper. At their separation she, the unknown and forever unnamed woman, vowed before God to remain faithful to Augustine until death. Augustine describes his own feelings: 'My concubine being torn from my side . . . my heart which clung to her was torn and wounded and bleeding' (*Conf.*, 6, 15 : 25).

It's not that I think of when I speak of Augustine's faults, but that he was very proud, and even arrogant. He was extremely sensitive to attacks. Jerome once called him a 'little upstart'. Augustine remained offended for a long time, even after Jerome had endeavoured to put things right. In himself, too, he was dependent on praise, perhaps even on flattery. At any rate it was very important to him what other people thought of him and his achievements—and this long after his conversion.

We should not, of course, be too hard on Aurelius Augustinus. Above all we must not forget how isolated this intensely sensitive and vulnerable man was all his life. His education was mediocre. It was that of an unimportant teacher in Africa. His philosophy to a large extent shows the marks of being self-taught. He was never able to master Greek, the language of culture of his time. He was an admirer of a middlebrow popularizer, Cicero, from whom he received the first decisive impulse in his inner life (by his reading of *Hortensius*). Throughout his life he had to contend with opponents who were, with the exception of Pelagius, unknown and charlatans. It must also be noted that he was very solitary in his intellectual world and his oppressive work, always circling round himself. Up to his death he never worked other than amid the hostile and ugly hum of personal and ecclesiastical enemies. These 'flies', as he called them, brought things to the point where the great part of his work took the form of apologetics. What bitterness against his enemies, but perhaps still more against himself and his own fate, rings through these words: 'They . . . begin to speak evil of me, many things which they know, many which they know not. For I was once, as the Apostle says, "foolish and unbelieving, and to every good work reprobate" . . . I was foolish and held by a perverse error, I deny it not; and in proportion as I deny not what has past in me, do I the more praise God, who has forgiven me. Why then do you, after the manner of heretics, leave the matter and concern yourself with the person? For what am I? What am I? Am I the Catholic Church? Am I the heritage of Christ diffused throughout all nations? Enough for me that I am in it' (*Enarrationes in Psalmos*, Ps. 36, III: 19).

I come here upon the fearful tragedy of this man's life, as if upon a warning signal for our own lives, the tragedy into which one sees more and more good men plunge today, the tragedy of self-righteousness, the sad fate of those who always want to know best. Need this

fate lie before us all? I pray God that we never be sub-
jected to it. Augustine, a spirit born to sympathy and
independence, let himself be driven along this tragic road.
The subjects of his writing, his intellectual combat, were
chosen for him by his enemies. He stood as if with his
back to the wall and was forced to oversharpen his formulations, and sometimes even his ideas themselves.
Because of these exaggerations he became, in the sub-
sequent history of the West, the occasion of almost all
schisms and heresies, or other tragic and dangerous
currents of thought. In the final, darkened years of his
life nothing would go right with him. He no longer had
a happy touch in his polemics and could no longer find
the proper Christian attitude towards an opponent, and a
restrained, humble, serious tone. Hard, sometimes exag-
gerated phrases and ideas on the sovereignty of grace,
the stumbling-block of the Cross, and reprehensibility of
the 'lust of the flesh' mark him out as a grim moralist
and theologian of sinfulness and human wretchedness. He
scarcely noted the publication of a hostile book before
reacting with uncalled-for speed—reactions of a kind that
are surprising in a man who otherwise worked patiently
through everything, and in whom everything was in harmony at a deeper level. Sure of himself (perhaps too sure)
and impatient for the fight, he would lie in wait for contradiction, hurl himself into the conflict, dictate and publish
a refutation, and that without taking the time to read
carefully through the work he was attacking, indeed—
alas—without reading it through to the end, or even without having had it in his hands at all. This happened to him
twice and he came to regret it.

Hence there gathered around Augustine's life an unwholesome atmosphere of polemics. Controversies, attacks, replies, refutations and clarifications dominated his writing and embittered his soul. His pupil Possidius, when he attached to his *Vita Sancti Augustini* a summary of the Master's works, could do no better than arrange them according to the succession of opponents Augustine had fought against. He gave nine headings. Augustine himself was much more detailed. At the end of his life he drew up a catalogue in which he distinguished eighty-eight erroneous doctrines.

In his more positive work also he ignored almost everything that had been thought before him and tried to think out everything anew, from within his own genius, on totally original lines, as if outside history, and denying any debt to the past. Yet he was a person whose whole longing was directed towards the 'harvest of God'. His inner attitude was 'ec-static': breaking away from himself, striding towards God.

Here regard must be had to the imperfect character of his experience of God. It was never more than a momentary happiness, passing like a flash of lightning. The vision is given only for an instant: 'And you beat back the weakness of my sight, streaming forth your beams of light upon me most strongly, and I trembled with love and awe' (*Conf.*, 7, 10 : 16) . . . 'And thus with the flash of one trembling glance it arrived at THAT WHICH IS . . . But I could not fix my gaze on that; and my infirmity being struck back, I was thrown again on my usual habits, carrying along with me only a loving memory of it . . .' (*Conf.*, 7, 17 : 23) . . . 'And while we [Monica and Augustine] were discoursing and panting after her [truth], we slightly touched on her with the whole effort of our heart

. . . and returned to vocal expressions of our mouth, where the word spoken has beginning and end' (*Conf.*, 9, 10 : 24).

By the compass of his lonely 'God and the soul alone' he wandered from one spiritual view of the world to another, and finally discovered in the Church the climate in which he found his natural environment, where he was able to grow.

There always remained in him, however—for he had stopped long enough in questionable and daemonic regions—something threatened, which later on, too, quickly revived and revealed the face of chaos, as soon as it strayed outside the regulating centre of the Church. Van der Meer, in his book *Augustine as Pastor*, has built up a picture of the Christian Augustine, out of hundreds of fragments, from letters and sermons, that has the effect of a mosaic, and amounts almost to a new discovery.

Augustine is presented as a man of his time who knew life, had himself been involved in many entanglements and had overcome them, had passed through error and finally come into the light. A hard-won peace marked the second part of his life and gave it a superiority that the first part had lacked. The search for God, however, had by no means slackened into tedium. Only it became more inward, patient, and modest. Augustine spoke of it in his later letters: 'My calm conceals much disquiet within itself' (*Epist.*, 213).

The more years that passed, and the more threatening the approach of old age, the more energetically we see Augustine defending his work and the leisure that union with God requires against being smothered by external activity. In 426 he handed over the greater part of his ecclesiastical functions to his successor, already named, the priest Heraclius. It was agreed that for five days in the week Augustine would be protected from all interruptions. He knew that his written work contained many imperfections and that he had much to make good. At the same time he was convinced that through his work he could be of use to the whole Church: both the Church of his own time and the Church of the future. I see him at the end of his life engaged in bringing his books into order, rooting out wrong judgments, correcting positions he had taken, excusing himself to his opponents, where he had been too hard on them, going through everything again, drawing up a catalogue and securing the preservation of his work in its purified form for posterity. His book of *Retractationes* is a work of inspired humility, a commitment of everything to God. For this book alone Augustine deserved to be canonized.

I have always found that the mere story of Augustine's life, above all of the upheavals in his life, is important as an example to every seeker after truth. It can be very fruitful on occasion to reflect on it, to make it the subject of meditation. The general facts are well known, so that it is unnecessary for me to note them here. I would rather consider those points in his career which I have found fruitful in the formation of my own thoughts, or which could still be so.

First: friendship. Augustine's spiritual life developed in the dialectic of attachments and encounters among friends. The figures of Alypius, Victorinus, Simplicianus, Ponticianus or, among his close relations, his mother Monica, his unnamed mistress and his son Adeodatus testify to a growing inwardness in human relations. These people were all witnesses of Augustine's spiritual struggles and his maturing. They too were drawn into the inner drama being played out between the soul and God.

As representative of many friendships I can cite here his ties with a friend of his youth. A melancholy beauty lies over this story. Since childhood the two had been bound together in a common striving for spiritual greatness. It is a type of search that can go with love for another person, indeed must do so, because it attains its own development only in such a love. Augustine remembers: 'In those years, when I first began to teach rhetoric in my native town, I had made one my friend, but too dear to me, from a community of pursuits, of my own age, and, as myself, in the first opening flower of youth. He had grown up as a child with me, and we had been both schoolfellows and playfellows . . . Yet was it friendship but too sweet, ripened by the warmth of kindred studies . . .' (*Conf.*, 4, 4 : 7).

It was a purely human friendship. Augustine emphasizes that it was not yet God who bound them together. Augustine was the stronger. He drew the young man away from his as yet insecure Christian faith into Manichaeism: 'From the true faith (which he as a youth had not soundly and thoroughly imbibed) I had warped him also to those superstitious and pernicious fables . . . With me he now erred in mind, nor could my soul be without him . . . You took that man out of this life, when he had scarce filled up one whole year of my friendship, sweet to me above all sweetness of that my life' (*ibid.*).

His friend, on the point of death, was baptized. Augustine mocked. His friend, however, inwardly transformed, 'With a wonderful and sudden freedom asked me, if I would continue as his friend, not to use such language to

G

him' (*Conf.*, 4, 4:8). Augustine was struck by the reality of holiness.

This friendship was surely the great emotional experience of his youth. Five chapters, the fourth to the eighth, tell of his sorrow: 'At this grief my heart was utterly darkened; and whatever I beheld was death. My native country was a torment to me, and my father's house a strange unhappiness . . . My eyes sought him everywhere, but he was not granted them . . . I became a great riddle to myself . . . And you abide in yourself, but we are tossed about in diverse trials. And yet unless we mourned in your years, we should have no hope left' (*Conf.*, 4, 4:9; 5:10).

Here different levels of experience lie one under the other. In Augustine's heart, where before there was only passion and, next to it, intellectual affinity, an inner depth was unlocked, of immeasurable shock in the face of final loss. Here there rose up, in a soul oppressed by sorrow, that reality to which hope belongs. The earthly pain did not cease to be pain. But at its highest point it unveiled its as yet unknown depth, that reality of the heart in which the 'God of hope' is already present. All Augustine's friendships were milestones on the way to eternity, on his ascent to God. This is an essential pointer to my philosophical attitude to life.

Secondly: his mother. Augustine's relationship to his mother, Saint Monica, was one of many levels. What really counted in Augustine's life were the powerful disturbances within his own soul. There is only one other person without whom his development is unthinkable—his mother. A large part of the *Confessions* is devoted to her. All accounts culminated in the wonderful conversation at Ostia Tiberina (*Conf.*, 9, 10 : 23–6) set in a grandly conceived account of Monica's inner life (*Conf.*, 10, 8 : 6; 13 : 37). There are also many shorter mentions and passing remarks that tell us still more of the way her life was intermingled with his.

Augustine, falling ill as a boy, asked his mother for baptism. But she withheld the sacrament from him because she feared that when he recovered he would not live according to the Christian commandments (*Conf.*, 1, 11 : 17). In adolescence, when Augustine's sexual life broke out strongly, his mother stood by warningly (*Conf.*, 2, 3 : 7). Thereupon—during his Manichaean period—a deep division set in between son and mother. Monica could only weep, but was comforted by a vision in a dream (*Conf.*, 3, 11 : 19). From a bishop to whom she turned for advice she received the reply 'God bless you, for it is not possible that the son of these tears should perish' (*Conf.*, 3, 12 : 21).

Augustine decided to go to Rome, and did not want his mother to go with him: 'I lied to my mother, and such a mother, and escaped' (*Conf.*, 5, 8 : 15). However, she followed him, first to Rome, then to Milan, where she put all her trust in Ambrose. Augustine struggled, made out that he could not speak with Ambrose. Monica then prevailed on Augustine to send away the woman in his life whom he loved and with whom he had lived for sixteen years. Looking at the way this happened I cannot avoid a certain impression of violence (*Conf.*, 6, 13 : 23 and 15 : 25). Scarcely had Augustine decided for the faith in the garden of Cassiciacum than he told at once and first of all his mother.

That Augustine, in the vision at Ostia Tiberina, dis-

cussed with his mother the deepest things in their relation
to God, that he carried out with her the religious movement towards God, the soul's ascent to its eternal home,
makes clear the whole force of her personality. Everything in Augustine's life was in some way accompanied
by his mother, whom her son, after painful frictions and
discord, learned to understand and honour ever more
unreservedly as a Christian, indeed as a reflexion of the
Church, protecting and accompanying him in a motherly
way. It is highly significant that in the *Confessions* the
picture of the earthly mother is often fused with that of
the Church (see *Conf.*, 1, 11:17; 5, 8:15).

The mother's life's work was now completed and she
could go in peace to fulfilment: 'One thing there was,
for which I desired to linger for a while in this life,
that I might see you a Catholic Christian before I died.
My God has done this for me more abundantly, that I
should now see you, despising earthly happiness, become
his servant: what do I here?' (*Conf.*, 9, 10:26).

I see how Augustine's tumult was ever more quietened
and how, in this quietening, he became ever more ripe
for word and deed. Without Monica's maternal soothing
Augustine might have been broken by his life. Perhaps
that applies to any kind of thinking.

Thirdly: Neoplatonism. It was Plato, and behind him
Socrates (transmitted through neoplatonists), who
brought Augustine to discover the metaphysical world and
its higher realities. The chapter on the uses and draw-
backs of Platonism, in its classical brevity, shows unmis-
takably that Augustine regarded Plato as a necessary, even
divinely willed preliminary to faith: 'Having then read
those books of the Platonists, and from them been taught

to reach for incorporeal truth . . . Upon these, I believe, you therefore wanted me to fall' (*Conf.*, 7, 20 : 26).

But can this personal statement be expanded into a universal property of God's saving will? If so, in what sense? I should maintain that Platonism in the form transmitted by Plotinus was for Augustine a more sublime temptation than Manichaeism, but an equally great one.

For ten years Augustine, the young Berber, was under the spell of the Babylonian Mani, and he escaped him only through the contrary spell of the Egyptian Plotinus. From materialistic dualism he overbalanced into spiritualistic monism, from the depravity of the senses into something that could easily enough have become depravity in a mystic technique of compelling God's grace by human effort, if the wise humanity of the Church had not led him to humble love of God and his neighbour, within the framework of the Christian community, filled with reverence.

Fourthly: his conversion. The eighth book of the *Confessions* describes Augustine's final breakthrough. He learned of the conversion of the Roman rhetorician Victorinus, who was concerned in the translation of Plotinus and whom Augustine revered. This example brought him to the point of decision. Shortly afterwards Augustine and his friends, assembled at Cassiciacum, received a visit from Ponticianus, a fellow countryman from Africa. He described the life of the hermit Antony and his followers. His courageous giving up of all things, from one moment to the next, confronted Augustine with the final Either/Or. While Ponticianus was speaking Augustine saw himself clearly in the sight of God : 'setting me before my face'. Augustine looked at his own life.

After a brief struggle all intellectual argument ceased. But the heart still resisted. The inward strain broke out in violence of speech and movement, but in vain. His face distorted, Augustine ran outside, and gathered up his whole being in a single declaration of readiness: 'Be it done now, be it done now.' His terrible obduracy gave way, and Augustine began to weep. Alypius, with marvellous tact, left him to this outburst of tears. Augustine, quite alone, now heard a child's voice chanting, 'Take up and read, take up and read.' Silently Augustine took up the Bible and read a sentence. He did not need to read further. It was no longer necessary. His face calm, he went to Alypius and showed him the place. Alypius read on and received the answer intended for him from God. Thereupon both went indoors to Monica and told her what had happened. She rejoiced, was triumphant and praised God (*Conf.*, 8, 5 : 10; 12 : 30).

I will not and cannot add any commentary on this event. It is the most sacred and mysterious happening in any Christian's life. Surely one day death will be found to be similar.

Various upheavals in Augustine's life have still to be considered, such as his resolve to become a monk, the ordination as priest imposed upon him by the people, the way in which, later on, he became conscious of the tragedy of his unhealthy polemics, and in decades of quiet labour completed, unseen, his non-polemical work, in which the grandeur of his soul attained its full expression: his books on the Trinity, the City of God, on Genesis, on the Psalms, on the Letter to the Romans and on St John's gospel. This and much besides should be thought and meditated upon if I am to draw full benefit for myself from Augustine's life and the sanctity of the great Father of the Church. However, what I have already written must be enough for the time being to draw the essential conclusions, stimulated by Augustine's example, for my own life. To this end I should like to give voice to Augustine's great longing, as he lived it in his life, and also in his tragic failures. Also, what is felt, but never fully realized, can point the way for me.

What is the result of this reflexion for me? I have leafed meditatively through the *Confessions*—that grateful record of a vital, battling, full-blooded life of stormy searching for God's truth. I have asked myself what yearning and what intimations of the just life are expressed there, and open a new future before me.

In the first instance, human life, in its concrete reality, is an opening of God to the world. The first, essential task of created existence consists in meditative experience of the meaning and manner of one's own transparency to God in the changing course of one's own life, as in Augustine's *Confessions*. Thus there comes about a thrust towards holiness and reverence for one's own destiny, bringing with it a unique, subjective relationship to God granted by grace to the individual and not replaceable by any concept. To find God in one's own life —that should be the first and most fundamental spiritual activity of a human existence truthfully lived out: 'loving memory' of God (*Conf.*, 17 : 23).

From that starting point a man should be able to come to a fundamentally new attitude to everything that enters this sacred area of his own life, and thereby becomes a herald of the absolute: to friendship and encounter, to sorrow and joy, to happiness and fate. Thus there comes about in a man's life a dedication of the soul, an application of piety to being in all its manifestations. But this is not merely occasional, something here and there, at a whim, but a primary instinctive gesture towards things, events and people. Affection for Being! The longing for such an attitude flows through the pages of Augustine's *Confessions*. A man should give himself up to the adventure of loving encounter with Being: 'I sought what I might love, in love with loving, and safety I hated' (*Conf.*, 3, 1:1).

These two attitudes—piety towards one's own life and piety towards Being—ought to guide us beyond themselves to testify and 'confess'. From us our fellow men must gain the possibility of understanding better their own life in God, so that they can join in our praise of God. The presence of God settling around us should take on in us the countenance of humanity, of goodness and goodwill towards men. It should be given a new understanding and illumination in the world by us, so that, overcome by the testimony to God of such transparent virtues, people call out: 'This is it which I love, when I love my God' (*Conf.*, 10, 6:8).

Then there arises, to use an expression of Teilhard de Chardin's, a *milieu divin* in the world, an area of peacefulness dominated by mildness, goodwill, sensitivity and absence of hostility. A Godlike spirit fills the living action of knowledge, thought and love. A new world is established which Augustine already understands as a promise of eternity, the eternity he tenderly called: *Cara aeternitas*—'eternity who art love' (*Conf.*, 7, 10:16).

Finally I want to ask myself Augustine's question— 'Do you think you can stick it to the end?' (*Conf.*, 8, 11:26). His answer is both modest and bold: 'So be it' (*Conf.*, 8, 11:25).

Teilhard and unity

Teilhard and unity

I have tried to define a 'spirituality' which will help the man of today in his often painful existence, and bear me up as I advance along the searching paths of thought. I have looked for an attitude in which both God and the world can be taken seriously. To be sure, we are all children of God. At the same time we are children of the earth. Together, these two approaches should give a lasting readiness to listen to God's summons in all life's situations, a capability for service to one's neighbour, and an openness of heart towards all that exists.

That apparently inauspicious beginning produced in me a spirituality of being present for God in the world, which can be put something like this :

On the one hand, man has to be quite open in everything relating to greatness. God always remains greater. Nothing satisfies us that is not God. Every fulfilment, therefore, here on earth as beyond in eternity, is the beginning of a further search. So the Christian must always stand in readiness for a new task from God. A holy dissatisfaction should dwell within him. All that has been achieved is, for that very reason, something that is closed for him. Only what has not yet been reached is worth tackling. Hence a man remains open for God and for his vocation in the world, and does not tie himself permanently to any chosen means. The greatest, the most beautiful, the most holy, is not great enough, not beautiful enough, and not holy enough for him. He won't be hemmed in by anything, however great. His longing is always greater than the greatest realization. The man is child of an ever-greater God.

On the other hand, this being a child in the sight of God, this openness to a greater fulfilment, man experiences as a 'child of the earth'. Therefore he must conceal the greatness of his eternal longing in the smallness of earthly realization. He has to seek his great God everywhere, even in the smallest and most inconspicuous things. Quietly and modestly, he must carry out the task God has intended for him, because in this smallness he finds the ever-greater God. The full measure of his being remains boundlessness. But he must enclose his longing within the smallness of what is attainable on earth. Whoever can combine the two in his life—boundlessness in great things and modesty in small—lives as a child of God and child of the earth.

'Not to be limited by the greatest, yet to remain within the smallest, that is divine', is Hölderlin's motto for *Hyperion*—which also draws on an epitaph of Ignatius Loyola's. Rest in restlessness, peace where there is no peace, acceptance of your own limitations together with ceaseless dreams of the unlimited, self-content with the least conspicuous, and always gazing towards perfection: such an attitude is the core of the spirituality I conceive for the man of today, and try to realize in my own life.

The whole tension between heaven and earth is drawn together in such a man. Heaven flows over into the earthly, and the earthly takes on an eternal content. I was surprised when I found just this attitude in Teilhard de Chardin.

That is the reason why he so fascinated me from the start. Teilhard de Chardin's attempt at a universal Christian interpretation of the world on an evolutionary basis has proved a decisive intellectual influence in the last ten years. There has been a multilingual dispute, ranging from enthusiastic endorsement to firm rejection, about his world-picture. I find the debate very petty, and prefer to try to lay bare the supporting and therefore hidden intentions behind Teilhard's thinking. I want to penetrate to that central point in Teilhard's inner personality where his scientific and religious statements are interwoven. Such an inquiry could create the basic pre-condition for an adequate interpretation of his work.

The search for the hidden purpose of a system of thought is a very difficult task. A great thinker never completely succeeds in saying what he basically wants to say. The constant lag of expression behind the original intention is one of the most painful experiences of profound thinkers. Heidegger justly says that a thinker's new teaching is in what is *not* said in his statements.

A full interpretation of a thought-system is possible only when the original but for the most part hidden tendency becomes visible behind the formulations. I have to grasp the inner structure of Teilhard's mind, examine his spiritual development and try to understand his achievement as a thinker from that point.

Is Teilhard's interpretation of the world teaching or testimony? It was very important to him that his readers should understand the words in which he presented his interpretation of the world. His essays and books contain no teaching in the sense of doctrine, but a testimony. They are less yet more than pure science.

In *The Heart of the Problem* he said of his work: 'It is a testimony to my life. A testimony I can all the less withhold since I am one of the few people who can give it.'

The opening lines of a short piece which is perhaps one of the most significant that Teilhard ever composed, *Let me Explain*, include the following statements: 'These lines will not put forward any theory, but trace the development of a personal discovery.'

I find something similar in *Human Energy*: 'The following pages are not immediately intended for the defence of any orthodoxy, either scientific or religious. They are simply trying to express in all sincerity a particular view of the world' (Teilhard de Chardin, *Let me Explain* [London, 1970] p. 154). But the most impressive formulation occurs in the opening lines of *My Universe*: 'These lines are not intended to provide any final explanation of the world. Nor are they intended to set up a general theory . . . I propose simply to set out my personal way and fashion of understanding the world.' These statements are evidence of a great intellectual honesty. They seem to offer the necessary key to an understanding of Teilhard's writings.

But who was the 'I' who is testifying in these writings? A man who was at once *priest and scientist,* and who endured this tension for a life-time. Teilhard de Chardin was fully conscious of his peculiar position. Over decades of specialized palaeontology he devoted the few hours between expeditions, or of rest after excavation, to writings in which he sought to create a synthesis between science and truth. He was deeply convinced that the sciences did not contradict revelation and led directly to Christianity.

From this conviction sprang his obligation to incorporate the evolutionary doctrine confirmed by his research into a theological treatment. Such a grafting of natural science into theology was then—and for some people is still—very bold indeed. Fifty years ago it would have been really difficult to define an objective connexion between natural science and theology. Teilhard de Chardin explains: 'The originality of my belief lies in its being rooted in two domains of life which are commonly regarded as antagonistic. By upbringing and intellectual training, I belong to the "children of heaven"; but by temperament, and by my professional studies, I am a "child of the earth". Situated thus by life at the heart of two worlds with whose theory, idiom and feeling intimate experience has made me familiar, I have not erected any watertight bulkhead inside myself. On the contrary, I have allowed two apparently conflicting influences full freedom to react upon one another deep within me. And now, at the end of that operation, after thirty years devoted to the pursuit of interior unity, I have the feeling that a synthesis has been effected naturally between the two currents that claim my allegiance. The one has not destroyed, but has reinforced the other. Today I believe probably more profoundly than ever in God, and certainly more than ever in the world.' (*Ibid.*, p. 154.)

What does this creative synthesis look like? First of all, Teilhard doesn't see creation and evolution as opposed realities. Instead the actual structure of evolution is the aspect of divine creative activity directed towards us. That is not a forcing of things into a pre-existing world, but an ascending development of things, out of the womb of the world, up to man. For Teilhard the world is like a gigantic process of development which for thousands of millions of years, step by step, and feeling its way forward through continuing complication and internalization of matter, ripens into its fulfilment. In this process man stands in the direct line of advance of all life.

Man, it is true, as Teilhard says (in Le groupe *zoologique humain*), 'is no longer, as it was once possible to believe, the unalterable centre-point of an already completed world, but—so far as our experience goes—the spearhead of the evolution of the universe. This comes about by means of an ever faster intensification of the complexity of matter, and at the same time a constantly increasing spiritual internalization'.

Man, says Teilhard, citing Julian Huxley in support, is 'evolution become conscious of itself'. He bears in himself the fate of the world. The will to life of the universe flows through him. Man himself, however, is not yet consummated. He is by nature a being in the process of becoming. This process of becoming man is not yet complete. Biologically and in spirit man is only at the beginning of his development. Teilhard follows other palaeontologists in speaking of fifty million years as the probable age of a zoological family of medium size. Even if one takes into account the powerful acceleration of evolution everywhere noticeable in humanity, we have some millions of years of possible future before us—a future that should be respected and not frivolously discarded.

Loyalty to humanity means for Teilhard, over and above loyalty to the past and the present, a loyalty to the future. Here the intensification of the human evolutionary drive has to be taken specially into consideration. Towards what future is mankind advancing? Teilhard de Chardin answers, towards the common 'axis' of the universe's development: that is, towards the unification of positive forces. As an evolving unity the universe increasingly converges, and tends to a single point. In man the evolutionary process is finally concentrated. With the breakthrough into the spiritual the whole development came together once and for all in man.

In the light of this consistently thought-out idea of evolution, our age appears as an absolute turning-point not only in human history but in the history of the entire cosmos. Individuals begin to strive towards each other. An ever-denser net of mental connexions is woven between them. The groups, units, nations, and families of nations and races begin to become ever more comprehensible to one another: more exposed, more open, more capable of living together. For Teilhard de Chardin this is a 'planetary rolling together', an all-embracing summing up of humanity. The development of life takes on a new impetus before our eyes. A new, higher synthesis of being is about to arise. Evolution is condensing into the single 'arrow' of an all-inclusive human community. But this convergence of mankind must not put in question the indispensable values of the human person. It must not suppress the highest 'achievement' of evolution—the human person—and lead to a form of totalitarianism. On the other hand a purely political and legal unification of mankind wouldn't be enough. It would never satisfy the demand for an organic unity awakened in the human soul. The ultimate convergence of the universe, which has been and will be further realized in mankind, cannot take place in mankind alone.

For Teilhard only one possibility remains: mankind

should become one through something that totally trans-
cends man, that at the same time is a person and thus
can assure man of his personal integrity, uniqueness and
freedom, but can also unite all men within itself: to use
the only true, practical name for it, through *God*. Teilhard says: 'At this point, it seems to me, the problem of
God arises for the science of evolution because only in
this way can evolution . . . maintain its progress: God, as
the converging point, the head of evolution.'

*   *   *

I have not yet expressed the ultimate and most characteristic point in Teilhard's understanding of the world. The
evolution of the world converges not simply upon God,
but upon the *God-man*. If mankind is to achieve the
final 'leap' of evolution, the leap of becoming one in and
with God, then the transcendental gulf between God and
man must be overcome. Then there must be someone who
is both God and man, a being of such richness that all
mankind can be integrated in him. Accordingly a God-
man is the unifying point, the 'Omega point' of evolution,
who lives in the state of resurrection, of all the per-
vading power of the spirit: a risen God-man who builds
up the fulness of his reality out of a mankind made one,
who alone makes this unification possible. Teilhard is
speaking here of the reality that Paul calls the 'pleroma',
the eschatological fulness of Christ. In this interpretation
of the world, evolution is a process in which Christ's incarnation and resurrection form the inner meaning of the
whole of world history. In this view nature does not
feature simply as an unmoved, fixed framework in which
the history of salvation is played out, but as an already

mysterious part of that history, as a process of maturing towards the Omega point, the 'cosmic Christ': that is, striving towards a condition in which God in Christ will be all in all.

To sum up this vision of the world I cannot do better than cite the introductory lines of *Let me Explain*: 'I believe the universe is an evolution. I believe evolution is striving in the direction of spirit. I believe spirit is perfected in the personal. I believe the perfection of the personal is the universal Christ.'

What is so fascinating in this view of the world, and remains even if you look at the overall design with reservations? Adolf Portmann, in a book on Teilhard, describes its unique effect: 'What fascinates us in this work is that it clearly goes beyond the narrow bounds of research. It is an attempt to unite what has been divided . . . Teilhard's effort to link together the most widely dispersed fields in a most intense intellectual process brings him very close to us.'

This is quite apart from the way individual elements in the synthesis are judged and its various formulations interpreted. Of course Teilhard's work has 'weak points', scientifically, philosophically and theologically. Even Teilhard's most resolute adherents could not assert that his picture of the world's development was a 'once-and-for-all' solution. The entire history of ideas speaks against this. All great ideas, on their first appearance, bear with them a train of peripheral errors. The greatness of the attempt almost necessarily means that the new structure is defective here and there. The decisive and all-important thing is the central ferment that brings about the effervescence and—step by step—the clarification. Teilhard de Chardin released a process of thought that now continues independently of him among Christian thinkers. Others will bring Teilhard's central contribution to its consummation.

The basic tendency of Teilhard's thought is deep-rooted in his uniqueness as a thinker. His scientific work is only one expression of the real thrust of his life. The most beautiful expression of this basic thrust is to be found in his experience of prayer, which speaks of a real commitment to the truth.

The first traces of this religious understanding of the world can be seen quite early in Teilhard's works. Particularly informative is a passage in his autobiographical essay which depicts Pierre's characteristic religious attitude to the world when he was seven : 'You should have seen me as in profound secrecy and silence I withdrew into the contemplation of my "God of Iron", delighting in its possession, gloating over its existence. A God, note, of Iron —and why iron? Because in all my childish experience there was nothing in the world harder, tougher, more durable than this wonderful substance. There was about it a feeling of full personality, sharply individualized . . . But I can never forget the pathetic depths of a child's despair, when I realized one day that iron can be scratched and can rust . . . I had to look elsewhere for substitutes that would console me. Sometimes in the blue flame (at once material, and yet so pure and intangible) flickering over the logs in the hearth, but more often in a more translucent and more delightfully coloured stone : quartz or amethyst crystals, and most of all glittering fragments of chalcedony such as I could pick up in the neighbourhood.'

For the young Pierre the material world contained an immeasurable mystery. He possessed a great power of concentration, of devoting himself to this mystery. Henri Brémond, like Teilhard himself from the Auvergne, was Pierre's teacher for years at the famous Jesuit college of Mongré. He depicts him as an extraordinarily quiet and withdrawn child: 'Pierre possessed a quiet passion, a jealously concealed passion, to which he totally devoted himself and which led him to live far from us: it was stones.'

What was going on in the heart of this young man I can only guess at, when I consider another account. It concerns an experience in prayer, of uncertain date. It occurred before Teilhard entered the Society of Jesus, and thus before he was eighteen. Teilhard describes it in his *Hymn of the Universe*: 'My gaze had come to rest without conscious intention on a picture representing Christ offering his heart to men. The picture was hanging in front of me on the wall of a church into which I had gone to pray . . . As I allowed my gaze to wander over the figure's outlines I suddenly became aware that these were *melting away* . . . When I tried to hold in my gaze the outline of the figure of Christ . . . these contours, and the folds of Christ's garment, the lustre of his hair and the bloom of his flesh, all seemed to merge as it were (though without vanishing away) into the rest of the picture. It was as though the planes which marked off the figure of Christ from the world surrounding it were melting into a single vibrant surface whereon all demarcations vanished . . . From this initial moment, moreover, the metamorphosis spread rapidly until it had affected everything. First of all I perceived that the

vibrant atmosphere which surrounded Christ like an
aureole was no longer confined to a narrow space about
him, but radiated outwards to infinity . . . All this
movement seemed to emanate from Christ . . . And it
was while I was attempting to trace the emanation to its
source . . . as my attention returned to the portrait itself,
I saw the vision mount rapidly to its climax . . . On the
unchanging face of Jesus there shone, in an indescribable
shimmer of iridescence, all the radiant hues of all our
modes of beauty . . . Beneath this moving surface . . .
hovered the incommunicable beauty of Christ himself'
(*Hymn of the Universe* [London, 1965] pp. 42–5 *passim*).

I regard this account as a key text in the thought of
Teilhard de Chardin. It shows clearly the early traces of
what he later advanced with great force: the whole life
of the cosmos is immersed in the reality of Christ. Christ
radiates forth to the remotest regions of this world. The
whole evolving cosmos is transparent, shot through and
shining, diaphanous with Christ. The holy is a condition
of our material world. These insights later assumed a
central position in Teilhard's mental world. He celebrated
them lyrically and with the highest religious dedication in
his '*Hymn to Matter*' :

Blessed be you, perilous matter, violent sea,
untameable passion . . .
Blessed be you, mighty matter, irrestible
march of evolution, reality ever new-born . . .
Blessed be you, universal matter, immeasurable
time, boundless ether . . . you who by overflowing
and dissolving our narrow standards of
measurement reveal to us the dimensions of God . . .

I acclaim you as the divine *milieu*, charged with
creative powers, as the ocean stirred by the
Spirit, as the clay moulded and infused with
life by the incarnate Word . . .
You I acclaim as the inexhaustible potentiality
for existence and transformation wherein the
predestined substance germinates grows . . .
I acclaim you as the melodious fountain of water
whence spring the souls of men and as the limpid
crystal whereof is fashioned the new Jerusalem . . .
I bless you, matter, and you I acclaim : not as
the pontiffs of science or the moralizing preachers
depict you, debased, disfigured—a mass of brute
forces and base appetites—but as you reveal
yourself to me today, *in your totality and your
true nature* . . .
Raise me up then, matter, to those heights . . .
until, at long last, it becomes possible for me . . .
to embrace the universe.

From this viewpoint Teilhard can speak of a 'cosmic
Mass'. For him the eucharistic mystery is simultaneously
and symbolically a universal event. What happens every
day in the Mass takes place mysteriously over thousands
of millions of years of cosmic development. During one
of his scientific expeditions in China in 1923 he spent
the Feast of the Transfiguration in the Ordos desert,
without bread, wine or an altar. There he celebrated the
'Mass over the world'. 'Since once again, Lord . . . in the
steppes of Asia—I have neither bread, nor wine, nor altar,
I will raise myself beyond these symbols, up to the pure
majesty of the real itself; I, your priest, will make the

whole earth my altar and on it will offer you all the labours and sufferings of the world . . . Receive, O Lord, this all-embracing host which your whole creation, moved by your magnetism, offers you . . . Lay on us those your hands—omnipresent—those hands which do not (like our human hands) touch now here, now there, but which . . . reach us simultaneously through all that is most immense and most inward within us and around us. Pronounce over this earthly travail your twofold efficacious word . . . Over every living thing which is to spring up, to grow, to flower, to ripen during this day say again the words: This is my Body. And over every death-force which waits in readiness to corrode, to wither, to cut down, speak again your commanding words . . . This is my Blood . . . Lord Jesus, now that beneath those world-forces you have become truly and physically everything for me, everything about me, everything within me . . . Glorious Lord Christ; the divine influence secretly diffused and active in the depths of matter, and the dazzling centre where all the innumerable fibres of the manifold meet; power as implacable as the world and as warm as life . . . It is to your body in this its fullest extension—that is, to the world become through your power and my faith the glorious living crucible in which everything melts away in order to be born anew; it is to this that I dedicate myself with all the resources which your creative magnetism has brought forth in me: with the all too feeble resources of my scientific knowledge, with my religious vows, with my priesthood, and (most dear to me) with my deepest human convictions. It is in this dedication, Lord Jesus, I desire to live, in this I desire to die.' (*Ibid.*, pp. 19–70 *passim*.)

Can matter be praised in more glowing terms? Can anything greater and more final be said of our world? Can one open oneself with greater respect to the workings of reality? In Teilhard's *Letters from a Traveller*, for example, there is the following passage, which is an entire meditation in itself: 'Today the sea is grey . . . Air and sea: a thick, living envelope, in which life swarms and hovers, as fluid and dense as the medium that holds it. Astonishment before the shape and the wonderful flight of the gull: how was that craft built? The worst failing of our mind is that we fail to see the really big problems simply because the forms in which they arise are right under our eyes. How many gulls have I seen, how many other people have seen them, without giving a thought to the mystery that accompanies their flight? . . . May God grant it to me always to hear, and to make others hear, the music of all things so vividly that we are swept away in rapture.' (*Letters from a Traveller* [London, 1962] pp. 122–3.)

My treatment of the features of Teilhard de Chardin's mind would be incomplete if I did not include the testimony of his friends. As representative of many I choose the evidence of Helmut de Terra in his *Memories of Teilhard de Chardin.* An agreeable raconteur, de Terra describes his expeditions with Teilhard in northern and central India, in Burma and in Java: 'I can still picture Teilhard vividly, his finely chiselled features wearing an air of transparency, his whole figure seeming to radiate concentrated spirituality . . . In his company one could always bank on a mental reflex which placed facts in a wider context . . . When scrutinizing fossils or artefacts, he gave the impression that he had somehow been involved in their formation, that he could grasp their underlying significance by means of a kind of inner eye . . . Let no one cherish any false illusions about the thoroughness of Teilhard's scientific research . . . He always insisted on accurate observation . . . The fact that Teilhard combined this analytical and critical faculty with a philosophical, profoundly religious and, one might say, almost mystical disposition will always remain one of my deepest and most abiding impressions . . . Enclosed by such a wilderness, I could always sense, in Teilhard's company, something of the mystical empathy with Nature which made him listen keenly for animal calls and sometimes provoked him to merriment . . . As we were picking our way through dense undergrowth in the shade of some huge trees, it suddenly occurred to me that we were in a noted game preserve and might well meet a panther at any moment. The idea of falling unarmed into the clutches of such a beast filled me with apprehension, for Teilhard as well as myself. Oppressed by such thoughts, I strode ahead of him, so firmly convinced that every rustle in the dark undergrowth denoted the presence of a lurking predator that it was on the tip of my tongue to suggest retracing our steps. When I turned back to communicate my fears, I saw my companion standing motionless, his eyes fixed on a thicket from which came a loud sound of snapping twigs. Involuntarily, I seized his arm. "This forest is like a sea of hidden life", he said, regarding me with veiled eyes. I should have know that, while I was giving way to fear, Teilhard simply felt like one creature among many.' (*Memories of Teilhard de Chardin* [London, 1964] pp. 67–142 *passim*.)

Finally I quote an ordinary, simple incident, that reveals

more of the man within than the subtlest analysis:
'Noticing that his feet were shod in light tennis-shoes, I
warned him to look out for poisonous snakes, which
were particularly numerous in the area. He glanced back
at me in surprise and said that he could feel the ground
much better in light shoes.' (*Ibid.*, p. 35.) That, expressed
in a single image, was the secret of Teilhard de Chardin.

In *La planetisation humaine* Teilhard once said of the
future: 'In the human community a new, extraordinary
element has appeared. You could call it *homo progressi-
vus*, that is, the man for whom the future means more
than the present. The first generations of this type of man
are already living among us. A clearly noticeable power
of attraction links these still scattered elements and brings
them steadily closer together. This power of attraction has
no limits, no impenetrable social, racial or religious
barriers. I have experienced a hundred times, and everyone confirms it, that whatever his country, his belief and
his social level, when I meet a man in whom this same
fire of expectation burns, there immediately comes about
a deep, total contact. It is quite inessential how we
formulate our hopes, according to our various styles of
upbringing and education. We feel ourselves simply
related. We are of the same humanity. Indeed we find
that even our disagreements bind us together. As if
there were a new dimension of life between us, from
heart to heart. For this phenomenon I see no other
explanation except that through the intellectual and social
upheavals that have shaken the world for a century and
a half, there has occurred a radical turning point within
the centre of the human substance. A growing self-
awareness of developing and moving forward, an irresis-

tible multiplication and unification of those forces in which the spirit of the future has awakened. These are the real driving forces of the unification of the world. Tomorrow they will constitute the human race.'

For Teilhard there is an inner connexion between the victory of Christ and the success of our human endeavour. The greater man is, the more humanity is united, self-aware and master of its own power, the more beautiful is creation, the more perfect our adoration, and the more will Christ find a 'mystical extension', a body worthy of the resurrection.

That was the vision of Teilhard in a world not shut off, but open, exposed to an eternal, divine consummation, which through us is transformed into a radiant universe transparent to God, into a divine setting. Expectation, hope, fearful, communal and active waiting for an end to the world (in Teilhard's sense I should really say, a *beginning* of the world) are a Christian duty, and perhaps the features of Christianity that distinguish it most clearly from all other religions. Teilhard de Chardin's work projects a transformation of Western man into a reality of world significance. He sketched out the basic attitude of the future, a future which—I hope—God will make great without denying the greatness of the world and of man. We can only hope that in us this expectation, which is perhaps closest to reality and certainly the most effective, will not be smothered at birth.

Epilogue

Epilogue

It would be superfluous and perhaps inappropriate to sum up the approaches described here. It must now be clear that the basic attitude is an 'openness of spirit'. If the spirit isn't open, our spiritual life stays cramped, or can't reach out beyond itself. If it is open, there are horizons before us which are not yet visible, but which 'openness' will certainly lead us to.

For my friends who read this very subjective though honest book I should like to say something about our attitude to the upheaval in the Church today. There is no cause for anxiety. God's Spirit is guiding the Church; something powerful has broken out. Our Christian life has been seized by fundamental impulses which are changing us inwardly.

God has 'ventured' something, and expects something of us: an attitude of mind that can be most simply described as 'the duty to be intelligent'. God challenges us today to ask questions, to push ahead into unknown territory, and to overhaul the conceptual apparatus of our message. The courage to do this isn't a liking for novelty, but the virtue of Christian intelligence. It consists in absolute honesty, in openness towards any kind of truth, and a resolute search for what is right. Here I have tried only to show what that spirit is and—I hope—to arouse the desire for it.

Acknowledgements

The author and the publishers acknowledge with gratitude the kind permission of the following to reproduce extracts from copyright translations: Messrs Wm. Collins & Sons for Teilhard de Chardin's *Let me Explain, Hymn of the Universe*, and *Letters from a Traveller*, and Helmut de Terra's *Memories of Teilhard de Chardin*; Penguin Books for Nietzsche's *Thus Spake Zarathustra*; and J. M. Dent & Sons for *The Death of Socrates*.